NECTAR OF KRISHNA'S NAME

Verses Kindler Publication.

Verses Kindler Publication.
Website: www.verseskindlerpublication.com

Nectar Of Krishna's Name

By: Mrs. Puja Chadha

ISBN:978-93-5605-578-0

SELF-HELP / SPIRITUAL 1st Edition
Price: INR 499/$22

Disclaimer

Nectar of Krishna's name is written by Puja Chadha.

The published work is the original contents of the author and she has done her best to edit and make it plagiarism-free.

The characters may be fictitious or based on real events but they are not meant to hurt anyone's feelings nor portray anything against any caste or system. Any resemblance of names of actual person, place or institute is purely coincidental to carry forward the story.

In case of any plagiarized write-up, the author is solely responsible for it, the publisher would not be responsible for it.

Preface

Like many other Hindu deities, Sri Krishna is referred to by various names. The numerous incarnations of Krishna and the numerous pastimes connected to Him are reflected in these names, known as Gouna Naams. Krishna's names are not mere designations; they encapsulate His divine qualities, His awe-inspiring deeds, and the profound cultural importance He holds throughout India.

One of the key explanations for Krishna's multiple titles is His complicated character. Krishna is not only revered as a God, but He is also viewed as a teacher, a lover, a hero, and a friend. Each of these roles reveals a distinct aspect of His character. The range of names He goes by also reflects this diversity.

For example, as a divine lover, He is called Madhava or Kanha, while as the supreme teacher, He is known as Jagadguru.

The wide range of local traditions and folklore throughout India is another factor contributing to the diversity of Krishna's names. Krishna's life is interpreted differently in different places, giving rise to regionally unique names and forms of worship. For example, Krishna is referred to as Panduranga or Vithoba/ Vitthala in Maharashtra, whereas Gopala is the name given to Him in Tamil Nadu, showcasing the intriguing diversity of Indian culture.

The various names for Krishna also have much to do with India's linguistic diversity. India is home to numerous languages and dialects. Hence, there are regional variations in how Krishna's name is spoken and referred to. He may be called Kannan or Keshava in South India, yet He may be called Kanha or Govinda in North India. These variants demonstrate the extent to which Krishna is ingrained in Indian culture.

Finally, different sects and traditions within Hinduism highlight various aspects of Krishna. This resulted in unique names and worship rituals. For instance, Krishna is frequently worshipped as Gopinath or Radha-Krishna in the Gaudiya Vaishnavism tradition, emphasizing His divine love for Radha. The variety of Krishna's names is further enhanced by how each sectarian perspective emphasizes a different facet of Krishna's deity.

Krishna has many names, and each one is a profound reflection of the linguistic, cultural, and religious diversity of India. These names carry significant meanings, representing the various roles that Krishna plays in the lives of His devotees. They also underscore the various ways that He is revered and honored across the country, highlighting the depth of His influence on Indian culture.

Table of Contents

Chapter 1: Introduction

Who is Bhagwan?

In our everyday life, we hear a lot about Bhagwan. Whether it's our grandmother praying in the morning, or if it's the beggar on the street, trying to emotionally ask for money in the name of God.

Do you really know what Bhagwan means?

In Hinduism, Bhagavan is the Supreme Being or God. He is the one who possesses all the divine characteristics and traits.

The word Bhagavan originally comes from Sanskrit words "Bhaga" meaning opulence and "van" meaning possessor. Hence, Bhagavan possesses all six opulence. He possesses all luxuries: riches, power, fame, beauty, wisdom, renunciation. He is supposed to be the ultimate Source of all things that exist. He is supposed to be the protector of the universe. He is the personification of unlimited and endless love towards His believers. In this regard, Krishna is believed to be Bhagavan because He signifies His exalted position as the ultimate and perfect representation of God.

Here is a more specific explanation of Bhagavan:

Bhagavan is love personified, compassion personified, with an added limitless love for His devotees, always ready to protect and guide them. He is the ultimate source of happiness and fulfillment and stands there to console and support us whenever needed.

Bhagavan basically denotes the supreme Origin of all creation. He is the creator, preserver, and destroyer of this universe. He is the ultimate source of all existence. He is who gives meaning and aim to our lives.

Bhagavan possesses all six opulence. As such, He is the richest, mightiest, most famous, most beautiful, wisest, and most renounced being in existence. He is the source of every manifestation of wealth, power, fame, beauty, wisdom, and renunciation.

Bhagavan is the guardian of the cosmos; He keeps the universe in order and protects it from harm. He is ultimately at the root of peace and harmony, and He is the one who always sees that justice is done.

Bhagavan represents the ultimate and perfect manifestation of the divine. He is the supreme being beyond human comprehension. He is the source of all goodness and truth. Bhagavan is worthy of our love, devotion, and worship. Whatever is necessary for this life and the life after, He can give. He alone can lead us on the path of eternal happiness and bliss.

Bhagavan is that entity for whom humanity exists. He is that target which we all are trying to reach. He will be our ultimate revival of all the longing or desires.

Bhagavan is the source from which all inspiration and motivation spring. He who alone can give the strength to overcome any 'problem'. He who alone can fill life with joy and meaning.

Bhagavan is the ultimate source of peace and happiness. Bhagavan is to give us the notion of inner peace and contentment. He helps find our true purpose in life.

Bhagavan is that ultimate source of wisdom and understanding who can help one to look at the world in quite a different way. He is the one who can help us develop our wisdom and understanding.

Bhagavan stands as the one source of beauty and grace. He is the one to help us appreciate this beauty in the world around us. He is the one to develop this beauty and grace within us.

Bhagavan is the ultimate embodiment of power and strength. And He alone can help us cross over any obstacle, face, or tide over any challenge. He alone can help us fulfill our aims.

Bhagavan is the source of all kinds of riches and prosperity. He stands between us and financial success. It is He who enables us to live the life of plenty.

Bhagavan is the one from whom reputation and fame arise; He is the one who can make our efforts successful, enabling us to live a life full of realization and satisfaction.

Bhagavan is the origin in everything that is good. He originates Love, Compassion, Wisdom, Beauty, Power, Strength, Riches, Prosperity, Fame, and Recognition.

Bhagavan is the aim of human life. Our souls are relentlessly going towards Him as He is to be reached ultimately. All our desires and longings will find fulfillment in Him alone.

Only Bhagavan can inspire and motivate us to reach the ultimate. He is the one who will give us strength when things beyond the power of human beings occur. He is the one who fills our lives with joys and meaning.

Attributes of Bhagavan

Do you know, there are 6 principal attributes that can help you understand who Bhagwan is?

These attributes signify his complete and infinite nature:

- Aishvarya: Supreme lordship and dominion.
- Virya: Strength and valour.
- Yashas: Fame and glory.
- Shri: Wealth and prosperity.
- Jnana: Knowledge and wisdom.
- Vairagya: Detachment and renunciation.

These attributes collectively describe an infinitely powerful, knowledgeable, detached, glorious, and wealthy being.

Bhagavan in Hindu Texts

When you come across the term "Bhagavan" what do you personally understand?

A few years ago, in my mind, every idol that adorned my temple... they were all God to me. All the deities were neatly arranged in a semicircle with a Diya lit at the center. I would always address them as Bhagwan. But then, I came into Krishna consciousness and learned about Krishna being the Supreme Being. He has declared Himself as Swayam Bhagwan in the Bhagavad Gita.

How do you relate to the idea of a Supreme Being who is both transcendent and immanent, personal, and impersonal?
When you hear about Krishna or other deities as "Bhagavan," do you view them as divine manifestations, or do you feel a personal connection to them?

Bhagavan, the Supreme Being, the source of all creation, is the heart that beats within the sacred texts of Hinduism. In every verse, He whispers the eternal truths, in every hymn, He is the melody of the soul. He is the compassionate guide, who walks beside us in times of joy and sorrow, the boundless love that cradles the universe. Through His divine words, we find solace, purpose, and the strength to surrender our burdens, knowing that in His embrace, we are forever cherished, forever home.

Bhagavad Gita:

In this holy book, Krishna frequently refers to Himself as Bhagavan. Lord Krishna declares His divine nature as the Supreme Being, or Bhagavan, in several places in the Bhagavad Gita. Some of the most prominent references are:

Bhagavad Gita, Chapter 10, Verse 8:
"Aham sarvasya prabhavo mattah sarvam pravartate" "I am the source of all spiritual and material worlds. Everything emanates from Me." This verse indicates that Krishna is the origin of everything, emphasizing His position as Bhagavan, the Supreme Godhead.

Bhagavad Gita, Chapter 7, Verse 7:
"Mattah parataram nānyat kiñcid asti dhananjaya" "O Arjuna, there is no truth superior to Me. Everything rests upon Me, as pearls are strung on a thread." Here, Krishna clearly declares that nothing is above or beyond Him, reinforcing His identity as the Supreme Being.

This reveals that Krishna is the All-Pervading Absolute Being. He shows that He includes all creation, maintenance, and destruction.

In the Bhagavad Gita, Lord Krishna reveals His all-pervading nature and His role in the creation, maintenance, and destruction of the universe in Chapter 9, Verse 10:

Bhagavad Gita, Chapter 9, Verse 10:
"mayādhyakṣeṇa prakṛtiḥ sūyate sa-carācaram hetunānena kaunteya jagad viparivartate"

"This material nature, which is one of My energies, is working under My direction, O son of Kunti, producing all moving and non-moving beings. Under its rule, this manifestation is created and annihilated again and again."

In this verse, Krishna explains that the material world operates under His supervision. He is the ultimate cause behind the cycles of creation and destruction, affirming His position as the All-Pervading Absolute Being.

Bhagavad Gita, Chapter 10, Verse 12:
"paraṁ brahma paraṁ dhāma pavitraṁ paramaṁ bhavān"
"You are the Supreme Brahman, the ultimate, the supreme abode and purifier, the Absolute Truth and the eternal divine person."

Although not part of the Vedas or Upanishads, the Bhagavad Gita is a key text; in which Krishna is recognized as the Supreme Personality of Godhead by Arjuna.

Srimad Bhagavatam:
This holy literature describes the supreme nature of Bhagavan. This book talks about the many incarnations (avatars) of Bhagavan Vishnu/Krishna and His heavenly pastimes.

In the Śrīmad Bhāgavatam, Lord Krishna speaks about His supreme position as Bhagavan in several instances. Some references where Krishna reveals His divine nature to Brahma:

Śrīmad Bhāgavatam, Canto 10, Chapter 14, Verse 32:
"nāhaṁ prakāśaḥ sarvasya yoga-māyā-samāvṛtaḥ" "I am not manifest to everyone, being veiled by My yoga-māyā. The foolish cannot recognize Me, the unborn and infallible."

This verse emphasizes that Krishna, though the Supreme Being, chooses to remain hidden from the understanding of the ignorant, underscoring His nature as Bhagavan, the source of all creation and the ultimate reality.

Śrīmad Bhāgavatam, Canto 1, Chapter 3, Verse 28:
"ete cāṁśa-kalāḥ puṁsaḥ kṛṣṇas tu bhagavān svayam"
"All of the incarnations mentioned here are either plenary portions or portions of the plenary portions of the Lord, but Lord Śrī Kṛṣṇa is the original Personality of Godhead."

This verse directly states that Krishna is "Bhagavan Svayam," meaning He is the Supreme Personality of Godhead, distinct from His various incarnations.

Vedas and Upanishads:
These ancient books explain the qualities and nature of the Supreme Being, also known as Brahman, Paramatma, or Bhagavan.

The identification of Krishna as Bhagavan in the Vedas and Upanishads is subtle and indirect, as these ancient texts often refer to the Supreme Being in more abstract or general terms. However, several scriptures do point towards Krishna or Vishnu as the Supreme Reality, which later traditions explicitly interpret as referring to Krishna.

1. Chandogya Upanishad (3.17.6):
Reference: The Chandogya Upanishad mentions Krishna as the son of Devaki. Although the text does not explicitly call Him "Bhagavan," this reference has been interpreted by later traditions as an acknowledgment of Krishna's divine nature.
Text: "Sa eṣa devakīputro vāsudevaḥ" ("He is indeed the son of Devaki, Vāsudeva").

2. Gopāla-Tāpanī Upanishad:
Reference: This Upanishad directly identifies Krishna with the Supreme Being and is one of the key texts that explicitly call Krishna "Bhagavan."
Text: "Kṛṣṇo vai paramam daivatam" ("Krishna is the Supreme Deity").

3. Mahānārāyaṇa Upanishad (Section 1, Verse 4-5):
Reference: Vishnu is identified with the Supreme Being, and since Krishna is an incarnation of Vishnu, this is often extended to Krishna in devotional traditions.
Text: "nārāyaṇaḥ paro'vyaktāt" ("Narayana is the Supreme reality beyond the unmanifest").

4. Rig Veda (1.22.20):
Reference: The Rig Veda speaks of Vishnu's supreme position, which in the context of Vaishnavism, is associated with Krishna.
Text: "tad viṣṇoḥ paramaṁ padaṁ sadā paśyanti sūrayaḥ" ("The wise always behold that supreme abode of Vishnu").

These texts are interpreted by followers of the Bhakti tradition, particularly Vaishnavism, as evidence that Krishna is indeed Bhagavan, the Supreme Being, even though the names Krishna or Bhagavan may not be directly mentioned in all cases. The Gopāla-Tāpanī Upanishad is the most explicit in identifying Krishna directly as the Supreme Being.

Aspects of Bhagavan

Have you ever wondered how God can be both everywhere and yet personally present in our hearts? The concept of Nirguna Brahman portrays God as an all-pervading, formless force, while Saguna Brahman shows Him with attributes, like Krishna or Vishnu, who interact with us personally. Can we grasp this duality, where the infinite becomes intimate, where the boundless takes form just to be with us?

The concept of Bhagavan in Hindu philosophy is rich and multi-dimensional, embodying both the Saguna (with form and qualities) and Nirguna (without form and qualities) aspects of the Supreme Being. These two aspects are fundamental to understanding how the Divine can be both personal and impersonal, relatable and transcendent.

Saguna Brahman: The Personal Aspect of Bhagavan

Bhagavan is frequently viewed by believers as the human face of the Supreme Being. As He possesses supernatural characteristics and attributes, qualities, and a manifest form. This makes Him personable and approachable. This concept is most vividly embodied in the personal deities, their particular forms, names, and pastimes, like Krishna, Rama, and Vishnu. These manifestations of the Divine are worshiped by millions of devotees for their relatable human-like qualities and their extraordinary, supernatural deeds.

We get the reference from The Bhagavad Gita
(Chapter 4, Verse 7-8): Krishna declares, "Whenever there is a decline in righteousness and an increase in unrighteousness, O Arjuna, at that time I manifest myself on earth. To deliver the

pious and to annihilate the miscreants, as well as to reestablish the principles of dharma, I appear millennium after millennium."

In the Ramayana, Lord Rama, an avatar of Vishnu, is depicted as the ideal king, husband, and son. His life on earth is filled with moral lessons and divine pastimes, such as His unwavering commitment to dharma (righteousness) and His love for Sita. Rama's story is an excellent example of Saguna Brahman, where the Supreme Being takes on a form and lives among humans, displaying divine qualities.

Nirguna Brahman: The Formless Aspect of Bhagavan

Nirguna Brahman refers to the Supreme Being without attributes or form. This is the infinite, formless, and impersonal aspect of God that transcends all material qualities. While Saguna Brahman makes God accessible and relatable, Nirguna Brahman represents the ultimate reality that is beyond human comprehension.

The reference is from the Upanishads. The Brihadaranyaka Upanishad (2.3.6): The text describes the nature of the Supreme as "neti neti" (not this, not this), suggesting that the ultimate reality is beyond all descriptions and cannot be fully understood or characterized by any human thought.

The Chandogya Upanishad (6.2.1), declares "Ekam evadvitiyam" ("He is One without a second"), emphasizing the non-dual, infinite nature of the Supreme that is beyond form and attributes.

In the Bhagavad Gita (Chapter 11), when Krishna reveals his universal form (Vishvarupa) to Arjuna, it transcends all material forms and qualities. Arjuna sees the infinite, formless, and terrifyingly majestic aspect of Krishna, which represents the Nirguna Brahman. This vision is so overwhelming that Arjuna requests Krishna to return to His more familiar, Saguna form as His charioteer and friend.

Integration of Saguna and Nirguna Brahman

Hindu philosophy often integrates both aspects, recognizing that the Saguna form is a way for devotees to relate to the Divine, while the Nirguna form represents the ultimate truth beyond all human understanding.

Reference from the Bhagavad Gita (Chapter 12, Verse 2-3): Krishna explains that while the worship of the formless (Nirguna) is higher and more difficult, worship of the personal (Saguna) form is easier for most people because it provides a tangible focus for their devotion.

In the Bhagavata Purana, the story of Prahlada exemplifies this integration. Prahlada, a child devotee, constantly worships Vishnu (Saguna Brahman). When Vishnu appears as Narasimha (half-man, half-lion) to protect Prahlada and destroy his demon father, Hiranyakashipu, He demonstrates both His personal form (Saguna) and His infinite, formless power (Nirguna), as Narasimha defies categorization within ordinary forms.

The duality of Saguna and Nirguna Brahman allows followers to connect with the Divine in ways that suit their spiritual inclinations. For some, the personal, loving forms of Krishna or Rama are central to their worship, while for others, the formless, infinite nature of Brahman represents the ultimate truth. Both aspects coexist within Hinduism, offering a comprehensive understanding of the nature of God as both immanent and transcendent.

Who is Krishna?

In Hinduism, Krishna is revered as the All-Pervading God. He is a central figure, worshipped as the Absolute truth. He is renowned for his compassion, intelligence, and divine playfulness. He was born in Mathura. However, He was raised in Vrundavan, where He performed wonders and enchanted everyone with His charisma. In the famous battle of

Mahabharata, He played an important role. He imparted the teachings of the Bhagavad Gita to Arjuna in Kurukshetra. Krishna is highly adored. He represents righteousness, joy, and love. His teachings and stories inspire millions. These highlight spiritual liberation, duty, and commitment. There are various reasons why Krishna is referred to as "Krishna" that are indicative of his holy nature and attributes:

- **Etymology/Origin:** "Krishna" comes from the Sanskrit word "Krish," which means "to attract." Krishna draws all beings towards Him through His captivating personality, the art of playing the flute, and divine pastimes (leelas).
- **Complexion:** The term "Krishna" literally translates as "dark" or "black." Due to His dark and lovely complexion, Krishna is so-called. This denotes His transcendental and mysterious character.
- **Divine Attributes:** Krishna possesses all the attractive qualities like fame, prosperity, renunciation, beauty, intelligence, and strength. The meaning of His name also tells that He is the Origin of all these divine qualities.
- **Cultural Significance:** "Krishna" is synonymous with joy, love, and devotion in Hindu culture and literature. He reflects His affectionate and playful relationships with His devotees, especially the gopis of Vrundavan.

Krishna is called "Krishna" as He has the potential to attract all beings with His divine qualities and His enchanting, dark complexion.

Why is Krishna called Bhagavan?

Krishna is known as Bhagavan because He has all divine attributes and opulence. As Bhagavan, Krishna is infinitely wealthy, powerful, renowned, beautiful, knowledgeable, and selfless. He is believed to be the ultimate source of all creation and the preserver of the universe. He is this, the Supreme Personality of Godhead. His supreme nature and unbounded compassion are demonstrated by His heavenly pastimes, profound teachings in the Bhagavad Gita, and loving interactions with his devotees. As a result, Krishna is regarded as Bhagavan, the whole and ideal embodiment of the divine, embodying every aspect of God.

Worship and Devotion

According to our Hindu tradition, we are divided into different groups, such as Vaishnavism, Shaivism, and others. Each group, though diverse, finds its way to connect with the Divine. Yet, isn't it beautiful how these different paths ultimately lead to the same truth? Whether one worships Vishnu or Shiva, at the heart of it, we are all united in our love for God, each journey reflecting the same light through different lenses. Doesn't this diversity only deepen the beauty of our faith?

- **Vaishnavism:** Vaishnavas are the followers of Vishnu and His avatars, such as Rama and Krishna. They focus on worshipping them.
- **Shaivism:** Here, people believe Shiva to be Bhagavan. They focus on worshipping Shiva.
- **Shaktism:** Followers refer to Bhagavan as Shakti, the Divine Mother.
- **Smartism:** Acknowledges the existence of several deities, such as Ganesha, Shiva, Devi, Surya, and Vishnu, and views them as distinct incarnations of the same Bhagavan.

Bhagavan and Devotees

Deep love, dedication (bhakti), and submission are the characteristics of Bhagvan's relationship with His devotees. Bhagavan is believed to be compassionate and caring towards His devotees. He is always ready to answer their prayers and assist them on their path to attain liberation (moksha).

In the Bhagavad Gita, Krishna presents three primary paths to spiritual realization: Bhakti Yoga (The path of devotion), Jnana Yoga (The path of knowledge), and Karma Yoga (The path of selfless action). These paths cater to different temperaments and spiritual inclinations, offering diverse routes to attaining union with the Divine.

1. Bhakti Yoga (The Path of Devotion)

This is the path of devotion where the devotees sing, chant, and meditate on the names and forms of Bhagavan. They try to establish personal contact with Him.

Reference: Bhagavad Gita, Chapter 12, Verses 1-2

Imagine Arjuna, a warrior prince, sitting amid a great battlefield, troubled by the chaos and conflict around him. He turns to Krishna, his charioteer and friend, and asks, Krishna.

Arjuna said, "O Krishna, how can I find peace amidst this turmoil? I wish to understand the true nature of devotion and the nature of those who worship You. What is the nature of the worship of the devotee who is absorbed in You?"

Krishna smiled gently and replied: "Arjuna, the path of devotion is your refuge. When you surrender to Me with a loving heart, focusing all your thoughts on Me, you will find a sanctuary of peace and a deep, abiding joy. Devotion is not just about rituals; it's about loving Me as your own and trusting in My guidance."

He continued: "Those who are always devoted and who worship Me with unwavering faith are the most dear to Me. Their devotion is pure, and they focus their hearts and minds on Me with great love."

2. Jnana Yoga (The Path of Knowledge)

Through jnana yoga, one attains knowledge and realization that Bhagavan is the ultimate reality. This path leads to liberation.

Reference: Bhagavad Gita, Chapter 4, Verse 33
Verse: "Knowledge is the highest form of knowledge, which leads to the realization of the Self. This knowledge helps in understanding the eternal truth about the Self and the Supreme Being."
Conversation: Consider Arjuna, seeking deeper understanding. He asks, "Krishna, how can I gain true knowledge and realize the Self?"

Krishna responds with a thoughtful look, "Arjuna, Jnana Yoga is the path of wisdom and understanding. By studying sacred texts, contemplating the nature of reality, and engaging in meditation, you will come to understand your true self, beyond the illusions of the material world. This knowledge reveals that you are part of the eternal essence that pervades everything, leading to liberation."

3. Karma Yoga (The Path of Selfless Action)

The path of selfless devotion to Bhagavan, which views all services as bringing the divine closer to humans.

Reference: Bhagavad Gita, Chapter 3, Verse 19
Verse: "Therefore, perform your duties efficiently and selflessly, for action is better than inaction. By working selflessly, you fulfill your obligations and contribute to the welfare of the world."
Conversation: Imagine Arjuna, pondering over his duties in battle. He questions, "Krishna, how should I approach my responsibilities?"

Krishna advises, "Arjuna, Karma Yoga teaches that you should perform your duties without attachment to the outcomes. Act selflessly, focusing on your actions rather than their fruits. When you work with this attitude, you purify your heart and align yourself with the Divine, fulfilling your role in the cosmic order."

Connecting the Paths

Each path offers a unique approach to spiritual growth, suited to different temperaments and life circumstances:

Bhakti Yoga is ideal for those who find solace and fulfillment in loving devotion and personal connection with the Divine.

Jnana Yoga appeals to those who seek understanding and wisdom, aiming to transcend the illusions of the material world through knowledge.

Karma Yoga is for those who wish to engage actively in the world, performing their duties with detachment and selflessness.

Krishna's teachings in the Bhagavad Gita offer a comprehensive guide to spiritual practice. Whether one is drawn to devotion, knowledge, or selfless action, each path provides a means to connect with the Divine and attain spiritual realization. Through these teachings, Krishna invites us to find the path that resonates with our inner nature and to pursue it with sincerity and dedication.

The Divine Glories of Krishna:

Shad-Aishwarya-Paripoorna

Majesty and Divine Form

Krishna's majesty (Aishwarya) is limitless. Throughout his life, he revealed his ultimate divine form, Virat Swaroop, multiple times. This form contains innumerable cosmic eggs (brahman) and their respective governors—Brahma, Vishnu, and

Mahesh—along with millions of suns, moons, and fire. When caught eating dirt at Brahmand Ghat in Gokul, Mother Yashoda saw this mighty form in Krishna's tiny mouth. Before the battle of Mahabharata, Krishna, as a royal ambassador of the Pandavas, revealed his divine form in the Kaurava court. On the battlefield of Kurukshetra, Krishna bestowed divine sight to Arjuna, showing his enormous form. After the Mahabharata war, while returning to Dwaraka, Krishna revealed his divine form to Uttank Muni.

Righteousness and Miracles

Krishna's righteousness (dharma) is also boundless. At six days old, He killed the demoness Pootana. In his infancy and childhood, He conquered many demons like Trinavarta. When Mother Yashoda tried to tie him to a stone mortar, all the ropes in Braj fell short by an inch.

Krishna assumed millions of forms during the Maharaas. On the way to Mathura, He revealed His Vishnu form, lying on the Shesh serpent, to Akroor. Narad Ji saw Krishna with all his 16,108 queens simultaneously. With two handfuls of puffed rice, Krishna endowed two lokas to Sudama. When Dushasana was disrobing Draupadi, Krishna descended as Ambaravatar (sari) to save her modesty. At 11, Krishna liberated His parents, held hostage by Kansa. He brought back the six sons of Devaki, who Kansa had killed. Krishna mastered all 64 branches of knowledge within 64 days and brought Sandipani Muni's dead son back from Yamlok as guru Dakshina. He washed the feet of Sudama, an ordinary Brahmin, with his tears. Krishna served the cows so devotedly that he earned the epithet Gopal (protector of cows).

Glory and Fame

Krishna's glory (yash) is unparalleled. Brahmas, Vishnus, Shankars, celestial gods and goddesses like Indra, Varuna, and Kubera venerate him. Great saints have worshipped Krishna for eternity. Jagadgurus like Shankaracharya, Nimbarkacharya, Ramanujacharya, and Madhvacharya, including the present Jagadguruttam Shri Kripalu Ji Maharaj, and famous Rasik saints like Hit Harivansh, Vyas, Lalit Kishori, Haridas, Nityanand, and Roop Goswami always sing his glories. Even in foreign lands, thinkers like Thomas Carlyle of England and Ralph Waldo Emerson of America have drawn inspiration from the Gita's philosophy. French author Jacolliot argued that the Holy Bible was written from the perspective of the Gita.

Prosperity and Wealth

Krishna's prosperity (shri) is immeasurable. He, whose consort is Maha Lakshmi, can immediately bestow ownership of entire worlds, as he did for Sudama.

Knowledge and Wisdom

The Gyan (knowledge) of Krishna is incomprehensible. He may impart divine wisdom and the knowledge to understand it, just as he did for Arjuna on the Kurukshetra battlefield.

Detachment and Renunciation

Krishna's detachment (vairagya) is profound. Despite killing Kansa, the ruler of Mathura, Krishna never desired to rule. He danced with millions of Gopis yet remained self-satisfied and free from lust. With 16,108 wives and 161,080 sons who later killed each other, Krishna remained untouched by grief.

Krishna embodies all these divine attributes in unlimited quantities, making him Shad-Aishwarya-Paripoorna (possessor of six opulences in full). The mentioned attributes are just a hint of His real glory, yet they sufficiently illustrate his divine nature. Understanding these attributes encourages devotion and reverence for Krishna, who is both majestic and accessible to his devotees.

Importance of names in Vedic tradition

In Vedic tradition, the idea of "rupa" (form) and "nama" (name) are closely related. A name is an essential component of the divine form. Names have great spiritual vibrations and deep implications. They represent the qualities and essence of the sacred. The celestial attributes and energy that deities represent are infused into their names. This makes them more than just labels.

According to the Vedic sages, a person can connect with divine energy by chanting or recalling the name of a deity, which is considered to summon the deity itself. Chanting these holy names aloud is an essential component of devotional life and is thought to have profound spiritual advantages.

Chapter 2: Krishna's Names

A: Significance of Krishna's Names

The importance of Krishna's name is profoundly illustrated in the Vishnu Sahasranama, a hymn that enumerates a thousand names of Vishnu (of whom Krishna is an incarnation). Each name in this hymn is a meditation on a particular attribute or deed of the Lord, serving as a means for devotees to remember and connect with His divine qualities.Lord Krishna is one of the many gods in the Vedic pantheon. He has been given many names, each representing a different aspect of His character, actions, and divine essence. The custom of giving Krishna several names aim to capture the many aspects of His divinity and provide devotees with various means of communication and ways to connect to Him.

The diversity of Krishna's names also speaks to the universality of His appeal. Different names of Krishna resonate with different devotees. Thus, Krishna allows His devotees to approach Him in a manner that is most meaningful to them. For example, a devotee who loves Krishna's childhood pastimes might be attracted to His name, "Balgopal" (child Krishna). On the other hand, one who admires His role as a warrior might prefer names like "Parthasarathi" (charioteer of Arjuna).

Achyuta

1. Achyuta (The Infallible One)

Leela: Guidance and support to Arjun

When the battle was being fought between the Pandavas and the Kauravas, Arjun faced moral dilemmas as he saw his own family on the other side. He was confused and was not ready to fight. Krishna was Arjun's charioteer. Seeing Arjun filled with grief and confusion showcased His role as Achuyta, the infallible one. Krishna provided him with guidance and support in these moments, and His wisdom was profound.

Krishna's discussion with Arjuna is known as the Bhagavad Gita, the song of God. This became a timeless scripture. It has been imparting profound spiritual and philosophical wisdom. Through His teachings, Krishna demonstrated His role as Achyuta. Achyuta is the one who is never shaken by doubts or failures. He provides steadfast guidance to those who are confused and need stability.

Arjuna was inspired and enlightened by Krishna's words. He found the strength to fulfil his duty. Krishna's role as the ultimate guide and protector of righteousness represents His infallible nature and is called Achyuta. Krishna reminded the devotees that He will always provide them with support and wisdom in the face of life's battles.

Adbhutah

2. Adbhutah (The Wondrous)

Leela: Giving Arjun divine eyes

One of Lord Krishna's most deep and amazing acts in the epic Mahabharata was to bestow upon Arjuna the ability to see his universal form, the Vishvarupa, or Divya Chakshu. This incident occurred on the Kurukshetra battlefield when Arjuna, paralysed by uncertainty and moral ambiguity, went to Krishna for help. In response, Krishna chose to show Arjuna His actual, cosmic form to alleviate any remaining questions and deliver the Bhagavad Gita, which revealed the essence of duty and righteousness.

Arjuna saw Krishna's limitless form—which had endless faces, arms, and heavenly symbols—through the Divya Chakshu. He perceived the past, present, and future all happening concurrently within this form. The vision was so powerful that it made Arjuna realise that Krishna was not only his buddy or charioteer but the Supreme Being who controls creation and destruction. This realisation overwhelmed Arjuna with both awe and horror.

Krishna's amazing deed of bestowing Divya Chakshu upon Arjuna is evidence of His divinity and capacity to transcend human limitations.

3. Ajanma (The Unborn)

Leela: The Birth of Krishna

Krishna is known as Ajanma, the Unborn. Despite His appearance in the material world, in a human body, He is eternal. He is beyond the cycle of birth and death. His birth itself is a divine Leela that underscores this paradoxical nature.

Devaki and Vasudeva were Krishna's biological parents. They were imprisoned by Kamsa. As Kamsa always had the fear of being killed by Devaki's eighth child. He ruthlessly killed all the six children born to Devaki. The seventh child was transformed into Rohini's womb and thus was saved.

Divine miracles took place on the night Krishna was to be born. The prison guards fell into a deep sleep. The heavy chains shackling Vasudeva broke, and the prison doors opened effortlessly.

In the middle of all this, Krishna appeared in His four-armed form. He wore divine ornaments and radiated an ethereal light. Devaki and Vasudeva saw the sight of the Supreme Personality of Godhead, who appeared as their child. The sight made them speechless. Happiness had no bounds. Krishna instructed Vasudeva to take Him to Gokul to Nanda Bhavan. He asked

Vasudeva to exchange Him with the newborn daughter of Yashoda and Nanda.

Vasudeva carried little Krishna across the furious Yamuna River, as Krishna instructed. The Yamuna parted to make way for the divine child. On reaching Gokul, Vasudeva exchanged Krishna with Yashoda's daughter. He carried the baby girl and returned to the prison with her. As soon as Kamsa attempted to murder the infant girl, she changed into the goddess Durga. She told him he was going to die soon. Despite being born as a child, Krishna's eternal nature as Ajanma is highlighted in this leela.

Though Krishna took birth as a child, this leela highlights His transcendental nature as Ajanma. He appears in the world not through the normal process of birth but by His divine will to perform His pastimes and uphold dharma.

4. Ajaya (The Unconquerable)

Leela: Battles of Krishna

Krishna's life was marked by His constant battles against evil forces, showcasing His nature as Ajaya, the Unconquerable. Kamsa was the tyrannical king of Mathura. His defeat by Krishna is one of the most significant events that tells us about Krishna as unconquerable, the Ajaya.

Kamsa kept on sending demons to Vrundavan to kill Krishna. Krishna exhibited extraordinary strength and bravery. He protected the people of Vrundavan.

<u>Demons Killed by Krishna:</u>

Putana:
Putana was a rakshasi (demoness) sent by the tyrant king Kamsa to kill the infant Krishna. She disguised herself as a beautiful woman and approached baby Krishna under the pretense of breastfeeding Him, but her milk was laced with deadly poison. However, Krishna, fully aware of her intentions, sucked not just the milk but also her life force, resulting in her death. By killing Putana, Krishna symbolized the destruction of falsehood and evil, even when it comes disguised in a seemingly beautiful form. Interestingly, despite

her evil intentions, Krishna granted Putana liberation (moksha) because, in her final moments, she had come into contact with the divine. This leela (divine pastime) highlights Krishna's ability to purify even the most sinful beings.

Sakaṭāsura:

Sakaṭāsura was a demon who took the form of a cart, planning to crush the infant Krishna while He lay underneath it. However, Krishna, just three months old, playfully kicked the cart with His tiny feet, reducing it to pieces and killing the demon instantly. This incident underscores Krishna's divine strength, which manifested even in his infancy.

Trinavarta:

Trinavarta was a demon who appeared as a whirlwind and carried Krishna high into the sky with the intent of killing Him. Krishna, however, increased His weight, making it impossible for the demon to maintain his grip. As a result, Trinavarta was choked and eventually fell to the ground, crushed by Krishna's divine power. This leela teaches the lesson that the divine can overcome any force, no matter how powerful it seems.

Vatsasura:

Vatsasura was a demon who assumed the form of a calf to mingle among Krishna's herd, intending to kill Him.

However, Krishna, aware of his identity, grabbed the demon by his legs, whirled him around, and hurled him against a kapittha tree, killing him. This leela symbolizes the protection that Krishna extends to His devotees, even in seemingly harmless situations.

Bakasura:

Bakasura, a crane demon, attempted to swallow Krishna. However, Krishna proved too much for the demon to handle. Krishna forced Bakasura to regurgitate Him, after which He snapped the demon's beak and killed him. This story emphasizes Krishna's role as the protector and savior of the innocent.

Aghasura:

Aghasura was a massive snake demon who attempted to kill Krishna and His friends by luring them into his mouth. Once inside, Krishna expanded His form, choking and bursting Aghasura from within. This leela shows Krishna's ability to confront and destroy evil, no matter how terrifying or overwhelming it may appear.

Vyomasura:

Vyomasura, the sky demon, abducted Krishna's friends and hid them in caves. Krishna, in His divine strength, defeated Vyomasura by hurling him to the ground and suffocating him.

This leela illustrates Krishna's power to bring light to darkness and rescue those in distress.

Śaṅkhacūḍa:
Śaṅkhacūḍa, a demon with a gem-studded conch on his head, tried to abduct the gopis (cowherd maidens) of Vrundavan. Krishna, however, intervened and killed him, then took the conch jewel as a token. This story reflects Krishna's protection of His devotees, especially the gopis who symbolize pure, selfless devotion.

Pañcajana:
Pañcajana was a conch-shaped demon who kidnapped the son of Krishna's preceptor, Sandipani Muni. Krishna ventured into the ocean, killed the demon, and rescued the boy. This incident not only highlights Krishna's role as the preserver but also underscores the importance of guru (teacher) in the Hindu tradition.

Shishupala:
Shishupala was Krishna's cousin and an incarnation of Jaya, a gatekeeper of Vishnu who was cursed to be born as a demon. Despite being given many chances by Krishna, Shishupala repeatedly insulted Him. During the Rajasuya Yagna of King Yudhishthira, Shishupala insulted Krishna 100 times, after which Krishna beheaded him with His Sudarshana Chakra.

This leela illustrates the concept of divine justice and the limits of tolerance.

Dantavakra:

Dantavakra, the incarnation of Vijaya (like Shishupala, also a gatekeeper of Vishnu), was killed by Krishna after the Kurukshetra war. He was one of the last demons Krishna defeated, symbolizing the end of evil forces that plagued the earth during Krishna's time.

Defeating Jarasandha:

Jarasandha, the king of Magadha, was a formidable enemy of Krishna. He harbored a deep hatred for Krishna due to the latter's slaying of Kamsa, Jarasandha's son-in-law. Jarasandha attacked Mathura, Krishna's city, 17 times with massive armies. Each time, Krishna defeated him, but instead of killing him, Krishna allowed Jarasandha to live, recognizing that his death would create a power vacuum that could lead to further chaos. Eventually, Krishna orchestrated Jarasandha's death by getting Bhima to challenge and defeat him in a wrestling match, thus restoring balance and justice.

From just 6 days old, Krishna faced numerous demons, battling for His very survival. This highlights His role as the protector of righteousness and embodies His name, Ajaya, as He remains invincible against the forces of evil.

5. Anandsagar (Ocean of Bliss)

Leela: Rasa Leela with Gopis

Krishna's is known as Anandsagar, the Ocean of Bliss. Rasa Leela with the Gopis of Vrundavan shows His nature as Anandsagar. This divine dance demonstrates the pure and ecstatic love between Krishna and His devotees. It transcends all material boundaries.

Krishna and the gopis of Vrundavan played Raas Leela in the forest on a full moon night. Krishna played His flute melodiously. It enchanted the Gopis to Him. They left everything behind, all their worldly duties and attachments. There were innumerable Gopis. So, Krishna expanded Himself to dance with each one of them individually. This made each Gopi feel uniquely cherished and loved.

The dance itself was a sublime manifestation of divine love. Here the Gopis represent the souls. They were absorbed in the bliss of Krishna's presence, dancing in perfect harmony with the Supreme Being. This leela represents the soul's complete oneness with the divine. It is complete and utter happiness.

Krishna's Rasa Leela is celebrated as the summit of divine love and bliss. It emphasizes his identity as Anandsagar.

6. Ananta (The Infinite)

Leela: The Vishvarupa (Universal Form)

Krishna is known as Ananta because of His limitless nature. He showed Arjuna His Vishvarupa, or Eternal Form, on the Kurukshetra battlefield.

Arjuna had moral dilemmas and doubts about fighting with his own family members. Just before the great battle of the Mahabharata could start. Krishna displayed His divine, boundless form to clear Arjun's confusion and teach him the deep lessons of life and responsibility.

In the Vishvarupa, Arjuna saw the entire cosmos encompassed within Krishna. He saw an endless array of shapes, faces, and limbs that demonstrated the divine's omnipresence and power. This shape demonstrated the cycles of creation and destruction, the infinite length of time, and the omnipresence of Krishna in a way that was both amazing and horrifying.

Arjuna came to understand the absolute might and boundless essence of the divine after being struck dumb by the majesty and infinitude of Krishna's universal form. He considered Krishna to be the everlasting, limitless reality that encompasses all things, rather than just his charioteer or buddy.

7. Bhaktavatsal (The Affectionate One)

Leela: Rishi Durvasa and King Ambarish

Bhaktavatsal means "the one who is affectionate to His devotees." It reflects Krishna's deep love and protection for those who worship Him with devotion.

King Ambarish, a great devotee of Lord Krishna, observed the Ekadashi fast with utmost devotion. On Dwadashi, the day to break the fast, Sage Durvasa visited Ambarish's palace. The king, respecting the sage, invited him to break the fast together. Sage Durvasa agreed but went to the river for his ablutions first.

The auspicious time for breaking the fast was running out, so on the advice of his priests, king Ambarish broke his fast by consuming a little water, which was both breaking and not breaking the fast according to rituals.

When Durvasa returned and realized what Ambarish had done, he was furious, feeling dishonored. He created a demon to kill Ambarish. However, King Ambarish remained calm and prayed to Krishna.

Krishna, true to His name Bhaktavatsal, immediately sent His Sudarshana Chakra (divine disc) to protect Ambarish. The

Chakra destroyed the demon and then turned towards Durvasa. Terrified, Durvasa fled to various deities for help, but none could save him from Krishna's Sudarshana Chakra. Ultimately, he sought refuge in Krishna.

Krishna told Durvasa that only Ambarish's forgiveness could save him. Durvasa returned to Ambarish and begged for mercy. The compassionate king prayed to Krishna, and the Sudarshana Chakra was withdrawn.

This leela highlights Krishna's unwavering protection for His devotees. Ambarish's faith and devotion brought Krishna's immediate intervention, showcasing His role as Bhaktavatsal. Devotees learn that Krishna is always there to protect and support them in times of need, provided their devotion is sincere and unwavering. This story underscores the importance of humility, forgiveness, and the divine love Krishna holds for His true devotees.

8. Bihari (The Enjoyer)

Leela: Pastimes in Vrundavan

Krishna is also known as Bihari, the Enjoyer. He was born in Mathur and was raised in Vrundavan. There He delighted His admirers with a variety of jovial and amusing activities. He performed numerous pastimes and captivated the hearts of the people of Vrundavan.

Krishna's joyful, lively, and loving activities in Vrundavan are a perfect representation of His Bihari character. They impart to followers the value of appreciating the divine presence in daily life and discovering joy in devotion.

Krishna is known by several names that include the word "Bihari," which generally refers to someone who roams or enjoys, especially in the context of His playful and enchanting activities in Vrundavan. Here are some of the popular names of Krishna with "Bihari":

Banke Bihari: This is one of the most famous names of Krishna, especially worshipped in the Banke Bihari Temple in Vrundavan. "Banke" means bent in three places, referring to Krishna's iconic tribhanga posture, and "Bihari" means the one who enjoys or roams, highlighting his playful nature.

Kunj Bihari: "Kunj" refers to the groves or small forests in Vrundavan where Krishna would play with the Gopis and His friends. "Kunj Bihari" thus refers to Krishna as the one who enjoys in these sacred groves.

Nikunja Bihari: This name also relates to Krishna's pastimes in the secluded groves (Nikunja) of Vrundavan, where He would spend time with Radha and the Gopis.

Vrundavan Bihari: This name highlights Krishna as the one who roams and enjoys the beautiful forests of Vrundavan, which is the main setting of His childhood and youthful pastimes.

Radha Bihari: This name emphasizes Krishna as the one who enjoys and delights in the company of Radha, His beloved. It underscores Their divine love and the playful, joyful interactions between Them.

Each of these names reflects Krishna's playful, loving, and enchanting personality, especially in the context of His divine pastimes in Vrundavan, where He is celebrated as the eternal lover and charmer of hearts.

9. Chaturbhuja (The Four-Armed One)

Leela: Appearance before Devaki and Vasudeva

When Krishna appeared before His parents, He assumed the appearance of Chaturbhuja, also known as the four-armed. He revealed to Devaki and Vasudeva His transcendent and holy essence.

It was captivating to see Krishna for the first time as a bright newborn child. He was holding the lotus, mace, discus, and conch in His four arms. In this celestial form, His true nature as Vishnu, the preserver and guardian of the universe, was revealed. His ultimate identity was enchanting at birth. This vision left Devaki and Vasudeva speechless and amazed, and they realized their kid was divine.

Krishna's Chaturbhuja form reassured them of His divine origin and His ability to protect them from Kamsa's tyranny. He then transformed into a normal human baby, allowing Vasudeva to carry Him safely to Gokul.

This leela illustrates how important it is to recognize and remember Krishna's omnipresence and omnipotence. Even while He engages in relatively unremarkable pastimes.

Damodar

10. Damodar (The Bound One)

Leela: Getting tied by mother Yashoda

One of the most endearing pastimes of Krishna is His leela as Damodara. Damodar means the one who is bounded. In this pastime Krishna is bounded by His mother Yashoda. Krishna has always been a mischievous child. Krishna once broke a pot of butter and fed it to the monkeys. His mother, Yashoda wanted to discipline Him. She then tried to tie Him to a grinding mortar.

She put in all her effort. Despite this, the rope always fell short by a few inches. Finally, with a loving sigh, she managed to tie Him up, not realizing that it was Krishna's divine will that allowed her to do so. The vision of the Supreme Being willingly bound by His mother's love filled the hearts of the villagers with awe and tenderness.

The name Damodara, meaning "one who is bound by the waist," came to symbolize the power of pure love and devotion. It showed that even the infinite and all-powerful can be bound by the sincere affection of a devotee. This leela underscored the intimate and personal relationship between the Divine and His devotees.

11. Dayanidhi (Treasure of Mercy)

Leela: Delivering the Elephant Gajendra

This leela, depicts Krishna as Dayanidhi, also called (Treasure of kindness). He saves the elephant Gajendra from a crocodile's jaws. This demonstrates His unending kindness and compassion for everyone.

Gajendra was an ardent follower of Lord Vishnu. He descended from elephants. One day he was enjoying a bath in the lake with his herd, when a crocodile attacked him. The crocodile grabbed his leg and tried to pull him into the lake. Even though Gajendra put immense strength, he was unable free himself from the crocodile's hold. After a long struggle, he realized that all his efforts were in futile. Gajendra, filled with devotion, prayed to the Supreme Lord for help. With his trunk, he plucked a lotus blossom and gave it to the heavens, earnestly praying to divine. In response to the earnest prayers of his devotees, Lord Vishnu manifested as Krishna. He quickly ascended on His celestial bird mount, Garuda to reach for help. With the swift disposal of the crocodile and the powerful Sudarshana Chakra (discus), He spared Gajendra. Filled with gratitude and fervor, Gajendra offered a heartfelt prayer to the Lord. Krishna granted Him liberation from the endless cycle of life and death, feeling satisfied by His devotion.

12. Devakinandana (The Delight of Devaki)

Leela: Krishna's Return to Mathura

Devakinandana, which means "Devaki's delight," is a term used frequently to describe Krishna and emphasizes His maternal protection and devotion to His mother. Raised in Vrundavan, Krishna eventually returned to Mathura to fulfill His destiny of destroying the demon Kamsa and meeting up with His real parents, Devaki and Vasudeva.

When Krishna initially came to Mathura, He battled along with Kamsa. He defeated several of his demons, displaying His unrivaled strength and divine authority. Balaram had a face off against the best wrestlers in Kamsa's army. They all were defeated. Krishna and Balarama released Their parents, Devaki and Vasudeva, from prison upon the death of Kamsa. Devaki was overcome with love and pleasure upon finally seeing her children after a long time apart. Krishna's homecoming confirmed His role as Devakinandana and brought His mother great joy and relief.

This leela emphasizes the close bond that Krishna has with His devotees, especially His mother, with whom He shares a deep affection. It also proves His dedication to righteousness and justice. He completes His heavenly duty and offers happiness and freedom to all who adore Him.

13. Dwarkapati/Dwarkadhish (Lord of Dwarka)

Leela: Establishing the Kingdom of Dwarka

Krishna as the Lord of Dwarka is often referred to as Dwarkapati. He was instrumental in the founding of the city of Dwarka. It serves as both a haven for His people and a hub of spirituality and culture.

Krishna, having defeated many enemies and coming under constant threat, decided to relocate His people to a safer area away from Mathura. He selected a secluded, deserted area of land on India's western coast. He used His heavenly abilities to order the building of the splendid city of Dwarka, which was practically impregnable due to its sea around it.

Dwarka was built with unparalleled architectural beauty and majesty. It developed into a lively city with gardens, palaces, and temples adorning it. Krishna ensured that wealth, justice, and peace were enjoyed by all His subjects as the compassionate ruler. Dwarka flourished as a center of devotion, scholarship, and culture under Krishna's direction. The populace prospered, and the city came to represent heavenly protection and rule.

14. Girdhari (The Lifter of Govardhan)

Leela: The Lifting of Govardhan Hill

Saving the people of Vrundavan from the wrath of the rain god, Indra is one of the most well-known exploits of Krishna, who is revered as Girdhari, the person who lifts off Govardhan Hill. This leela emphasises Krishna's protective duty and His divine capacity for miracles.

Every year, the people of Vrundavan offered an annual sacrifice to Indra, seeking his blessings for timely and adequate rainfall for their crops. Instead, the peasants were persuaded by young Krishna to worship Govardhan Hill. The hill which gave them access to vital resources. The peasants carried out their rites at Govardhan Hill after being convinced by Krishna's words. This infuriated Indra.

Being angry Indra decided to punish the residents of Vrundavan. He unleashed torrential rains and thunderstorms upon the village. The rain was so intense that it threatened to flood Vrundavan. It destroys everything. When Krishna witnessed the panic and distress among the villagers He decided to act upon it.

Krishna lifted the entire Govardhan Hill with His little finger, with a playful smile. He held it as if holding an umbrella. He asked all the villagers and their cattle to take shelter beneath the hill. He held up Govardhan Hill for seven days and seven nights. He thus provided protection and refuge to everyone. The storm raged on, but the people of Vrundavan remained safe and dry under the hill.

Indra realized that Krishna was no ordinary mortal but He was the Supreme Personality of Godhead. Indra stopped the storm and approached Krishna with humility. He acknowledged Krishna's divinity. He begged for forgiveness for his arrogance. Krishna demonstrated His limitless power, divine protection, and compassionate nature by lifting Govardhan Hill.

This leela of Girdhari shows Krishna's omnipotence. It shows His role as the ultimate protector of His devotees. It emphasizes the importance of faith and devotion in the divine. It even shows Krishna's ability to intervene miraculously to safeguard His followers.

15. Gopala (The Beloved Cowherd)

Leela- The happiness provider to His followers

Krishna, the cowherd kid was often referred to as Gopala. He gave the people of Vrundavan unending happiness. His flute tunes delighted everyone and brought harmony and happiness into the air. Krishna would bring the cows to the pastures each day. His laughter resonated through the fields and created a divine melody in the air.

One evening, Krishna was sitting behind a banyan tree and playing His flute as the sun was setting. The cows and the gopis (cowherd females) were drawn to Him by His melodious singing. As they got lost in the heavenly ecstasy of Krishna's presence, they sang and danced. The meaning of His name, Gopala, was embodied in every note He played on His flute. It is a proof of His love for all living things.

During this happy festivity, the gopis came to understand that Krishna's love knew no bounds and was for everyone. His name, Gopala, became a byword for heavenly bliss and love, serving as a constant reminder of the unbreakable tie that is found between the divine and His followers.

16. Govinda (The Protector of Cows)

Leela: Killing of Arishtasursur

As a young boy, Krishna led the cows to graze when the morning sun illuminated the meadows in the picturesque village of Vrundavan. The villagers lovingly referred to Him as "Govinda," which means the guardian of cows. The cows recognized His celestial presence and followed Him with an unexplainable loyalty.

One day, a terrible demon named Arishtasursur, disguised himself as a monstrous bull. He charged into Vrundavan, intending to wreak havoc. The villagers fled in terror. However, Krishna stood firm, His eyes were radiating calmness. As Arishtasursur charged, Krishna caught him by the horns and wrestled him to the ground with ease. The earth trembled, but Krishna's strength was unmatched. With a mighty roar, He vanquished the demon, restoring peace. The villagers, witnessing this divine act, realized the true significance of the name Govinda. Krishna was not just their protector but the sustainer of life itself. His leela gave assurance to the safety and well-being of all creatures, especially the beloved cows. From that day, the name Govinda echoed with deeper reverence, symbolizing Krishna's role as the guardian of life and nurturer of nature.

17. Gyaneshwar (The Knowledge Giver)

Leela: Spreading of knowledge

The Bhagavad Gita's portrayal of Krishna and Arjuna's conversation on the Kurukshetra battlefield is considered as one of Lord Krishna's profound leelas (divine pastime). It highlights the significance of His name Gyaneshwara, the Lord of Knowledge. This is an ageless discourse that clarifies the fundamentals of spiritual understanding and divine wisdom. It also tells us about Krishna's function as Gyaneshwara.

Lord Krishna is a charioteer of Prince Arjuna's during the epic battle of Mahabharata. The battle took place due to the conflict between the Pandavas and the Kauravas. Krishna plays the role of a guide to Arjun. Just before the fight begins, Arjuna refuses to hold his bow and arrow. He was pushed into the uncertainty about his warrior's duty. Arjuna was hesitant. He was ready to take up sanyas and beg for alms rather to fight against his relatives and gurus.

Krishna recognized Arjuna's inner turmoil and His wavering determination. He begins to impart divine wisdom and knowledge to His friend and devotee. This pivotal moment marks Krishna's manifestation as Gyaneshwar, the Lord of Knowledge. He is one who dispels ignorance and helps His devotees to travel to the path of righteousness by imparting spiritual enlightenment.

Krishna elucidates the concept of dharma. He tells him about his righteous duty. He informs him the importance of performing one's prescribed duties without attachment to the results. He emphasizes that every individual has a duty to fulfill according to their role in society. He tells him that performing these duties selflessly contributes to the welfare of all.

Krishna teaches yoga of Devotion and Knowledge. He expounds on various paths of yoga. These paths include karma yoga (the yoga of selfless action), bhakti yoga (the yoga of loving devotion), and jnana yoga (the yoga of knowledge). He reveals that these paths are interconnected and lead to the realization of the Supreme Truth. Krishna encourages Arjuna to develop devotion (bhakti) towards Him as a mean to attain spiritual liberation and union with the divine.

As a result of Krishna's lessons as Gyaneshwara, Arjuna undergoes a significant spiritual development. He regains his resolve to carry out his warrior's task. He even achieves clarity of vision, and overcomes his uncertainties. Arjuna understands that his mission in the conflict is to defend righteousness and restore dharma, and this is not just to fight a physical battle.

Throughout the centuries, both experts and seekers have found resonance in the conversation between Krishna and Arjuna found in the Bhagavad Gita. It functions as a timeless text that offers spiritual direction and universal truths that are relevant to every facet of life. Krishna's incarnation as Gyaneshwara emphasizes how crucial divine insight and knowledge are for navigating the challenges of everyday life and achieving enlightenment.

Krishna's leela in the Bhagavad Gita as Gyaneshwara epitomizes His position as the Supreme source of wisdom and enlightenment. It emphasizes His heavenly knowledge and compassion, pointing humanity in the direction of self-realization, devotion, and righteousness.

18. Hari (The Remover of Sins)

Leela: Transformation of Dhundhkari

In a nearby village, there lived a sinful man named Dhundhukari. His life was filled with wrongdoings, and he was feared and despised by all. One day, a sage told him about the name Hari, which means "the remover of sins." Desperate for redemption, Dhundhukari began to chant the name of Hari with sincere repentance.

Through the power of Krishna's name, Dhundhukari experienced a profound transformation. His heart, once filled with darkness, began to fill with light and peace. He gave up his immoral habits and committed his life to helping others. The villagers recognized the name Hari's magical ability after being amazed by his transformation.

This leela showed how Krishna, in his incarnation as Hari, has the power to purify the hearts of even the most fallen souls, His name provides them with a way back to divine love and redemption. The name Hari came to represent hope to everyone looking for pardon and a fresh start.

19. Hrushikesha (Master of the Senses)

Leela: Krishna as the Charioteer in the Mahabharata

Krishna, the master of the senses is often referred to as Hrushikesha. He vowed not to pick up weapons in the entire battle. Yet He was an important character in the Mahabharata, especially as Arjuna's charioteer and adviser.

This leela highlights Krishna's mastery over the senses and His capacity to provide heavenly knowledge. When Arjuna was fixed with moral perplexity and anguish, he looked to Krishna for direction during his darkest hour. As Hrushikesha, Krishna took charge of the situation and delivered the immortal spiritual treatise.

Krishna's discourse in the Bhagavad Gita where revealed His divine form (Vishvarupa) to Arjuna, reaffirmed His position as the Supreme Being. This vision further solidified Arjuna's faith and determination to fulfill His dharma as a warrior.

This leela highlights Krishna's role as the supreme guide and teacher. He who can provide clarity and wisdom in the face of confusion and turmoil. It teaches you the importance of self-control. He provides spiritual knowledge, and unwavering devotion to the divine.

20. Jagadish (Lord of the Universe)

Leela: Krishna's Universal Form

Krishna is respected as Jagadish, the Lord of the Universe. This title highlights his absolute sovereignty over the entirety of creation. Krishna's revelation to Arjuna of his universal form (Vishvarupa) was a powerful example of this feature of His personality. Upon Arjun's request Krishna granted Him heavenly vision (as narrated earlier) to see His Vishvarupa, a form that included the entire cosmos.

Arjuna saw a beautiful, breathtaking scene. Krishna took on a huge, all-encompassing form that had an infinite number of faces, eyes, arms, and weapons. Arjuna saw the entirety of creation—past, present, and future.

He saw the countless ways that the divine could appear, the various gods and celestial creatures that exist, and the life-cycles of the dead. This vision was both horrifying and beautiful. Arjuna witnessed the cosmic dance of creation and annihilation, in which Krishna was the source of all things. The brilliance of this form is so powerful and magnificent, like the light of a thousand suns, overwhelming Arjuna with its sheer.

Krishna's omnipresence, omnipotence, and omniscience were revealed in His universal form. It strengthened his role as the universe's ultimate sustainer and controller. Arjuna was profoundly affected by this discovery, and he bowed down before Krishna and identified Him as Jagadish, the Lord of the Universe, with a great deal of respect and awe.

This leela, instills sense of humility and devotion in His followers by emphasizing the significance of acknowledging the divine presence in all facets of life and the universe.

21. Jagannath (Lord of the Universe)

Leela: The Ratha Yatra Festival

This festival's origin can be traced back to a time when Krishna, Balarama, and Subhadra all desired to travel on a symbolic journey to Vrundavan. Krishna took the decision after sensing the deep love and devotion of the people of Vrundavan. This holy leela is performed during the Ratha Yatra, which represents Krishna's unbreakable relationship with His devotees.

In this form, Krishna is mainly worshiped at Puri, Odisha. There he is known as Jagannath, the Lord of the Universe. One of the most important celebrations honoring Lord Jagannath is the Ratha Yatra (Chariot Festival), which draws attention to His all-encompassing character and enduring attractiveness.

The Ratha Yatra honors Lord Jagannath's annual journey (yatra) from His temple to the Gundicha Temple which is revered as Their aunt's home. He travels there along with His siblings, His elder brother Balabhadra (Balarama) and younger sister Subhadra. The deities are placed on grand chariots and pulled through the streets of Puri by thousands of devotees.

They represent the cosmic chariots of the universe. The act of pulling the chariots signifies the devotees' participation in the divine journey. It fosters a sense of unity and devotion. The festival attracts millions of pilgrims from around the world, transcending cultural and geographical boundaries.

Devotees passionately dance, chant the holy names of Krishna. They sing hymns throughout the Ratha Yatra. The air is full of joy and spiritual energy. It reflects Lord Jagannath's compassion and love for all people. This celebration highlights Krishna's position as the Lord of the Universe who is available to everyone, irrespective of caste, religion, or social standing.

The Jagannath Ratha Yatra leela emphasizes Krishna's inclusivity and willingness to interact with all His devotees. It highlights the significance of group worship, communal adoration, and the celebration of divine love that binds all people together under Krishna's all-encompassing rule.

22. Janardan (One Who People Pray To)

Leela: Rescuing Draupadi

Krishna is known as Janardan which means the one to whom people pray. He demonstrated His protective and compassionate nature in the leela where He rescued Draupadi. Draupadi. In the game of dice she was, during her humiliation in the Kaurava court.

The Pandavas were called by Kauravas for a game of dice, known as *Chaucer*. After the Pandavas lost everything in a deceitful game. Duryodhana the eldest of the Kauravas ordered his younger brother Dushasana to bring Draupadi to the court. Draupadi the queen of Hastinapur and the wife of the five Pandavas, was dragged into the court and subjected to public humiliation. Dushasana attempted to disrobe her. Draupadi, finding herself in a situation of extreme distress and helplessness, fervently prayed to Krishna. She called out to him for protection.

Touched by her sincere devotion and fervent request, Krishna responded immediately. As Dushasana pulled at her sari, Krishna miraculously extended the length of the cloth. He provided Draupadi an infinite supply of clothes. No matter how much Dushasana tugged at it, the sari never let up, it just kept coming. He protected Draupadi's modesty and dignity.

Krishna's miraculous intervention exemplified His duty as Janardan, the guardian of all who seek His shelter. Draupadi's steadfast trust in Krishna and His prompt answer to her prayer shows His close connection between a devotee and the divine.

This leela emphasizes the value of sincere devotion and trust in God, especially during hard times. It gives devotees peace of mind. As we pray to Krishna with a clean heart, He will always be there to protect and uphold them. Krishna's manifestation as Janardan emphasizes His willingness to grant His followers' requests for divine protection and grace.

23. Kamalnath (Lord of Lakshmi)

Leela: Marriage to Rukmini

Rukmini is thought to be an incarnation of Lakshmi and Kamal is another name for the goddess Lakshmi. This leela celebrates the divine union of Krishna with Rukmini. Krishna's status as a consort of Lakshmi. It shows His attributes as a loving and protective spouse. Thus, Krishna is also known as Kamalnath.

Rukmini was the princess of Vidarbha. She was deeply in love with Krishna. She thought He would be a perfect husband. Her brother Rukmi had other plans regarding her marriage. He had arranged her marriage to the strong but arrogant prince Shishupala. Rukmini, who was desperate to marry Krishna, secretly wrote a letter to Him. In the letter she confessed her love and requested Him to save her.

Krishna always gets moved by the devotion of devotees. Rukmini's devotion and sincerity also moved Him. Krishna decided to intervene. On the day of her marriage to Shishupala, Krishna along with his brother Balarama, arrived in Vidarbha. As Rukmini prepared to visit the temple of goddess Parvati, Krishna seized the opportunity. He swiftly lifted Rukmini onto His chariot and drove away. Everyone present there was shocked. Shishupala and Rukmi got angry and they decided to take revenge from Krishna and Balram.

A fierce battle took place between Krishna's forces and those of Shishupala and Rukmi. Krishna emerged victorious. He defeated Shishupala and subdued Rukmi. He then brought Rukmini to His kingdom, where They were married in a grand ceremony.

This leela of Kamalnath highlights Krishna's qualities as a loving and devoted husband. His willingness to go to any extent to protect and honor His beloved. It also shows the deep bond between Krishna and Lakshmi, symbolized by His marriage to Rukmini.

The leela teaches the importance of sincere devotion and the divine protection that comes with it. Rukmini's unwavering love and faith in Krishna were rewarded with His divine intervention and eternal companionship. This story illustrates the ideal relationship between the divine and the devotee. It is characterized by love, devotion, and mutual protection.

24. Kamalnayan (Lotus-Eyed One)

Leela: Enchanting the Gopis

Krishna is known as Kamalnayan, the one with lotus-eyes. He captivated the gopis of Vrundavan with His beauty and the melody of His flute. It celebrates His playful relationships with the gopis (cowherd maidens). The emphasis of this leela is on Krishna's dual roles as the epitome of celestial beauty and the ultimate lover.

The gopis were great devotees. They were mesmerized by Krishna's charm and presence. Of all His pastimes, Rasa Leela is the most captivating and well-known. When Krishna played the flute in the fall, He created a tune so divine that the gopis were drawn from their houses into the forest to sing and dance with Him.

In the moonlit forest of Vrundavan, Krishna danced with the gopis, each feeling as though Krishna was dancing with her alone. This miraculous feat demonstrated Krishna's ability to be personally present with each devotee, catering to their individual love and devotion.

The Rasa Leela symbolizes the ultimate union between the soul and the divine. Krishna's lotus eyes, which reflect His compassion, love, and beauty, enchanted the gopis and drew them into a state of divine ecstasy. The gopis, representing the purest form of devotion, surrendered completely to Krishna, experiencing the bliss of His divine presence.

This leela of Kamalnayan highlights the importance of divine love and the transformative power of Krishna's beauty. It teaches that true devotion transcends worldly attachments and leads to a direct and personal experience of the divine.

Krishna's interactions with the gopis also illustrate the concept of bhakti (devotion) as a path to spiritual fulfillment. The gopis' unwavering love and surrender to Krishna serve as an example of the highest form of devotion, where the devotee seeks nothing but the joy of being in the divine presence.

25. Kamsaantaka (The Slayer of Kamsa)

Leela: The Defeat of Kamsa

Krishna killed Kamsa and He liberated the people of Mathura from a cruel ruler. This heroic act was celebrated and He was called Kamsaantaka. This leela depicts Krishna's role as the divine protector. He is the upholder of righteousness.

Kamsa, the tyrant king of Mathura, was a constant threat to his subjects. To save Krishna from Kamsa, He was secretly taken to Gokul where He grew up with other herdsmen. But His destiny called Him back to Mathura. When Krishna and His brother Balram were mature enough, to fulfill the prophecy they decided to confront Kamsa.

They traveled to Mathura. They had decided to liberate their parents and the people of Mathura. Accompanied by His brother Balarama, Krishna entered Mathura. They faced Kamsa's numerous wrestlers and finally Krishna killed Kamsa.

They entered Kamsa's arena where a wrestling match was going on. Krishna effortlessly defeated Chanura and Mushtika, Kamsa's strongest wrestlers. Finally, He leaped onto the royal dais, and caught hold of Kamsa. He dragged him down into the arena. With just a single blow, Krishna killed Kamsa. Thus, His parents and the people of Mathura were free from tyranny.

His bravery and His path of righteousness not only liberated Mathura but also reinstated Krishna's grandfather as the rightful ruler. The people of Mathura celebrated their freedom and the end of Kamsa's tyranny.

The leela of Kamsaantaka showcases Krishna's role as the enforcer of dharma (righteousness). It illustrates the victory of good over evil. It shows the importance of divine intervention in restoring justice. Krishna's fearless and decisive actions serve as an inspiration for devotees. It highlights the importance of courage, righteousness, and unwavering faith in the divine.

26. KaliyaNartana (The Serpent Killer)

Leela: Subjugation of the serpent Kaliya

One of the most dramatic and heroic leelas of Krishna is the subjugation of the serpent Kaliya, known as Kaliya Nartana. This event further solidifies Krishna's divine prowess and His role as the protector of Vrundavan.

The Yamuna River, which flowed through Vrundavan, was once inhabited by the venomous serpent Kaliya. His poison contaminated the water, causing the surrounding area to become lifeless and desolate. The residents of Vrundavan were terrified of Kaliya and avoided the river.

One day, while playing with his friends, Krishna noticed that a calf had drunk the polluted water and had fallen unconscious. Determined to protect His beloved village, Krishna decided to confront Kaliya. He climbed a large Kadamba tree and, to the astonishment of His friends, leaped into the river.

As Krishna splashed into the water, Kaliya emerged, hissing, and coiling around Him, trying to crush Him. Unfazed, Krishna began to grow, making it impossible for Kaliya to hold Him. He then climbed onto Kaliya's multiple heads and began to dance gracefully. With each step, Krishna's divine energy subdued the serpent, forcing Kaliya to acknowledge His divine power.

Kaliya's wives emerged, pleading for mercy and promising that Kaliya would leave the river and never return. Krishna, compassionate as ever, forgave Kaliya and instructed him to go to Ramanaka Island, where he would live peacefully without harming anyone.

This leela of Kaliya Nartana not only displays Krishna's immense strength and fearlessness but also His compassion and willingness to protect those who are innocent. His dance on Kaliya's heads is symbolic of His mastery over the forces of darkness and chaos, reaffirming His role as the divine protector.

27. Keshav (The Slayer of Kesi)

Leela: The Slayer of Kesi

The tranquil life of Vrundavan was once threatened by a fearsome horse demon named Kesi, sent by the malevolent King Kamsa. Kesi's presence caused chaos and fear among the villagers. Krishna is known as Keshava as He killed Kesi. He took it upon Himself to confront the demon.

People who were standing there were terrified when Kesi charged towards Krishna. Their hearts were struck with fear. But Krishna, calm and resolute, faced the demon with divine confidence. With His incredible agility and smartness Krishna dodged Kesi's attacks. He ultimately thrust His arm into the demon's mouth and expanded it to an immense size. This choked the best and took away his life.

The villagers who witnessed this miraculous feat, praised Krishna for His bravery and strength. The name Keshava, once again resonated with the triumph of good over evil. It became a reminder of Krishna's role as the protector and savior, vanquishing darkness and restoring peace.

The other reason for Krishna being called Keshav. It has a significant meaning related to his divine attributes.

Keshav (केशव) can be broken down into two parts: Kesha, meaning "hair" or "hair lock," and V, which is derived from Vishnu, one of the principal deities of Hinduism. Thus, Keshav generally means "one who has beautiful hair" or "one with glorious locks of hair."

In artistic depictions of Krishna, His hair is often shown in elaborate styles, reflecting His royal and divine status. The name Keshav aligns with these representations and helps devotees focus on His majestic and divine appearance.

Krishna is called Keshav due to His beautiful and divine hair, which symbolizes His supreme beauty and divine nature. This name reflects not only His physical appearance but also His overarching glory and majesty as the supreme deity in Hinduism.

28. Ladoo Gopal (Baby Krishna)

Leela: The Stealing of ladoos

It is one of the most beloved and endearing names of Lord Krishna, particularly when He is depicted as a child. The name "Ladoo Gopal" comes from the image of baby Krishna holding or being offered a ladoo (a sweet ball made of flour, sugar, and ghee) in his tiny hands. This name highlights His childhood innocence, charm, and the love that devotees, especially mothers, feel for Him as a child.

The leela associated with Krishna as "Ladoo Gopal" originates from His early years in Gokul, where He was raised by Yashoda and Nanda Maharaj. Baby Krishna was known for His mischievous nature and His love for butter, sweets, and other delicacies prepared by the gopis of Vrundavan.

One day, Yashoda, Krishna's foster mother, prepared a large quantity of ladoos for a festive occasion. As she arranged the sweets in a large container, she noticed that the number of ladoos seemed to be decreasing mysteriously. Yashoda could not understand where they were disappearing, as she had not yet offered them to anyone.

Suspecting Krishna's usual mischief, she decided to catch Him in the act. Yashoda pretended to leave the kitchen but secretly watched from a hidden corner. As expected, little Krishna, drawn by the irresistible aroma of the ladoos, sneaked into the kitchen. He reached out with His tiny hands to grab as many laddus as He could, stuffing them into His mouth and savoring the sweetness.

Caught in the act, Krishna looked at His mother with innocent, wide eyes, His cheeks puffed with the sweets He had been eating. Seeing her little Gopal enjoying the ladoos so much, Yashoda could not help but smile, her heart melting with love for her mischievous child.

From that day, baby Krishna became affectionately known as "Ladoo Gopal," symbolizing his innocence and the love and devotion of his devotees. The name reminds devotees of the simple joy and divine sweetness that Krishna, in His child form, brings into their lives. It also reflects the love and affection Yashoda and the Gopis had for Him, always wanting to feed Him and keep Him happy.

The name "Ladoo Gopal" holds a special place in the hearts of devotees, particularly in the tradition of worshiping Bal Gopal, or baby Krishna. Many households in India keep a small idol of Ladoo Gopal and care for it like a real child, offering sweets, dressing Him up, and even singing lullabies. This practice symbolizes the deep personal and loving relationship devotees have with Krishna, seeing Him not just as a deity but as their own child, who brings immense joy and love into their lives.

29. Madan (God of Love)

Leela: Attracting the Gopis

Krishna is the deity of love. He is called Madan, revered for His divine beauty. He leaves His enchanting effect upon the gopis (cowherd maidens) of Vrundavan. Krishna is emphasized in this leela as the ultimate lover and the personification of alluring and beautiful beauty.

The gopis fell madly in love with Krishna because they were enthralled with His humorous demeanor and divine attractiveness. Krishna's divine love reached its zenith in the Rasa Leela, one of the most famous leelas.

The enchanting music that Krishna's flute generated one autumn night drew the gopis from their houses into the Vrundavan jungle. They assembled around Krishna to start the Raas, a dance of the heavens that represented the perfect union of the soul with the divine. Every gopi had the impression that Krishna was dancing just with her. This showcases His ability to be personally present with each devotee. This miracle leela serves to emphasize His status as the all-powerful, all-pervasive lover.

It is commonly said that Krishna is more beautiful than the god of love, Cupid (Madan). He who enthralled the gopis with His presence. His melodic voice, endearing grin, and lotus-like eyes exuded a sense of divine love and bliss. The ultimate level of devotion is symbolized by gopis.

They completely surrender themselves to Krishna. Thus, they experience the bliss of His divine presence.

This leela of Madan highlights the importance of divine love and attraction. It teaches that true devotion transcends worldly attachments. It results in an up-close and intimate encounter with the divine. The idea of bhakti, or devotion, as a route to spiritual fulfillment is shown by Krishna's relationships with the gopis. In this path, the devotee desires nothing but the bliss of being in the divine presence.

30. Madhava (The Lord of Spring)

Leela: Playing flute in the forest

Vrundavan's season of rebirth and beauty was ushered in by Krishna, also called Madhava, the lord of spring. There were flowers in bloom, lots of greenery, and a happy, fragrant environment when He arrived. A festival honoring the heavenly presence of Krishna and the splendor of nature was held one spring.

Krishna performed a flute concert in the middle of a wooded forest. He was wearing garlands made of fresh flowers. The beauty of nature around Him seemed to magnify His divine radiance. The gopis danced around Him, their hearts bursting with the joy of spring and Madhava's presence as they were adorned in vivid hues.

Krishna talked on the importance of spring as a season of rebirth and growth as they danced. He reminded them that just as nature rejuvenates, their hearts too should renew their love and devotion. The name Madhava came to symbolize the eternal freshness and beauty of divine love, inspiring the devotees to keep their faith ever blooming.

31. Madhusudan (Slayer of the Demon Madhu)

Leela: Defeating the Demon Madhu

Krishna, also known as Madhusudan, vanquished the monster Madhu to demonstrate His strength in protecting the universe from bad forces. This leela focuses on Krishna's role as the ultimate warrior who vanquishes evil and upholds dharma, or righteousness.

According to legend, the demons, Madhu, and Kaitabha, had emerged from Lord Vishnu's ear wax. These powerful demons created havoc in the universe. They challenged the gods and caused widespread destruction. The gods went to Vishnu and pleaded for help. Vishnu manifested as Krishna in response to the gods' cries for help. He assumed the identity of Madhusudan to fight the demons.

There was a fierce battle which lasted for several days. Krishna fought with Madhu and Kaitabh and demonstrated His supreme strength and fighting skills. Initially the demons were overconfident, then they realized Krishna's divine power. They negotiated for their lives. However, Krishna was determined to restore peace and order. Hence, He continued the battle with relentless vigor.

In the end, Krishna defeated Madhu and Kaitabh. He liberated the universe from their oppression. This triumph demonstrates His function as the defender of the dharma and the vanquisher of evil forces. Thus, Madhusudan represents Krishna's everlasting dedication to upholding morality and shielding His followers from danger.

This Madhusudan leela emphasizes the significance of divine intervention in upholding cosmic justice and order. It reassures them that Krishna is the ultimate protector and is always present. He will always triumph over evil and defend morality. By invoking Krishna as Madhusudan, devotees seek His protection and strength to overcome their own inner demons and adversities.

32. Manmohan (Attractor of the Mind)

Leela: Krishna's Playful Pastimes in Vrundavan

Krishna is known as Manmohan, one who attracts the mind. He has the power to captivate the hearts and minds of everyone in Vrundavan. With His divine charm and playfulness, everyone gets mesmerized.
This leela emphasizes Krishna's irresistible beauty and His ability to draw devotees into a state of divine love and bliss.

Krishna has always been a playful boy. He was the center of affection and attention because of His charming presence and lively nature. The entire town loved Him for His mischievous acts, including stealing butter and pulling practical pranks on the gopis. Initially, the gopis and other villagers were annoyed by Krishna, but in the end, Krishna's purity and heavenly humor won their hearts.

The leela that describes Krishna's hobby of stealing butter is among the most charming ones, as it depicts His position as Manmohan. The gopis tried to hide their butter, but Krishna always managed to find a way out to reach the butter pot and steal it. His actions would often leave the gopis both exasperated and enchanted, unable to resist his divine charm.

Krishna always mesmerized everyone by playing His flute. The gopis would follow the sweet melody of His flute into the jungle. There they would meet Krishna, who would be waiting to greet them with merriment and playful interactions. His flute playing represented the divine call that draws all the souls of the devotees to the divine presence.

Krishna's playful pastimes in Vrundavan emphasize His function as the one who can capture the mind like a magnet. He draws His devotees into a pure state of love and devotion. His interactions with the villagers and gopis teach us the value of discovering happiness and the divine presence in day-to-day activities. By invoking Krishna as Manmohan, devotees seek to experience the bliss of His divine charm and to be constantly drawn to His divine presence.

33. Manohar (One Who Steals the Mind)

Leela: Stealing of the Gopis' Clothes

Krishna is referred to as Manohar, the one who is a mind-stealer. He performed many leelas that demonstrated His ability to captivate and enchant his devotees.

One such leela is the one in which Krishna playfully steals the gopis' clothes. This emphasizes both His profoundly spiritual relationship and His mischievous nature.

The gopis would bathe in the Yamuna River, leaving their clothes on the bank of the river. One day, the ever playful and mischievous Krishna decided to teach humility and devotion to the gopis. Krishna gathered their clothing and climbed a nearby tree as they were taking a bath.

When the gopis looked around for their clothes, they realized their clothes were missing. They saw Krishna sitting on the top of the tree. He was holding their clothes. The gopis felt embarrassed and helpless. They pleaded Krishna to return their clothes. Krishna, with a mischievous smile, asked them to come out of the water and take their clothes from Him.

Initially they were reluctant. However, the gopis eventually stepped out of the water, humbling themselves before Krishna. This act of surrender symbolized their complete devotion and willingness to set aside their ego for the sake of their love for Krishna. Krishna was pleased with their humility and devotion. Hence, He returned their clothes and blessed them with His divine presence.

Manohar teaches profound spiritual lessons about surrender, humility, and the intimate. Krishna's playful act of stealing the gopis' clothes highlights the importance of letting go of one's ego. It even emphasises to leave material attachments to cultivate true spiritual love and devotion.

By invoking Krishna as Manohar, devotees seek to have their minds captivated and purified by His divine presence. This leela shows the transformative power of Krishna's charm. It showcases the relationship between the devotee and the divine. It even depicts the deep spiritual connection that arises from sincere devotion and humility.

34. Mayura (One Adorned with Peacock Feathers)

Leela: Krishna's Dance with the Peacock Feathers

Krishna, known as Mayura, the one adorned with peacock feathers, is often depicted with a peacock feather in His crown, symbolizing His divine beauty and connection to nature. One of the most enchanting leelas associated with this name is Krishna's dance with the peacock feathers, showcasing His divine grace and harmony with nature.

In the lush forests of Vrundavan, Krishna's presence brought life and joy to all beings, including the animals and birds. The peacocks, in particular, were enchanted by Krishna's flute-playing and His divine aura. Whenever Krishna played His flute, the peacocks would gather around Him, spreading their vibrant feathers in admiration.

One day, as Krishna played His flute, the peacocks began to dance in joy. Moved by their devotion and beauty, Krishna joined their dance, gracefully moving with them and adding to the splendor of the scene. The peacocks, in their gratitude, offered Krishna their most beautiful feather, which He graciously accepted and placed in His crown.

This leela of Mayura highlights Krishna's harmonious relationship with nature and His ability to bring joy and beauty wherever He goes. His dance with the peacocks symbolizes the divine dance of life, where all of creation participates in the joyous celebration of the divine presence.

The peacock feather in Krishna's crown also represents His role as the supreme artist, whose divine creativity manifests in the beauty and harmony of the natural world. By invoking Krishna as Mayura, devotees are reminded of the importance of living in harmony with nature and recognizing the divine beauty in all of creation.

This leela teaches that true devotion involves a deep appreciation for the beauty and grace of the natural world, and a recognition of the divine presence that pervades all of creation. Krishna's dance with the peacock feathers serves as a reminder of the joy and harmony that come from living in alignment with the divine.

35. Mohan (The Enchanter)

Leela: Krishna's Butter-Stealing Antics

Krishna, known as Mohan, the enchanter, is celebrated for His irresistible charm and enchanting personality that captivated the hearts of all who encountered him. One of the most beloved leelas highlighting this aspect of Krishna is His butter-stealing antics in Vrundavan, which demonstrates His playful nature to shower happiness to His devotees.

As a child, Krishna's love for butter was well-known throughout the village. He would often sneak into the homes of the gopis (cowherd women) and steal freshly churned butter. Despite their best efforts to hide the butter, Krishna, with His mischievous ingenuity, would always find a way to locate and enjoy his favorite treat. The gopis, though initially annoyed, could not help but be enchanted by Krishna's charming antics.

One day, the gopis decided to catch Krishna in the act. They placed the butter pots in high, seemingly unreachable places, thinking this would deter him. However, Krishna, along with His friends, devised a clever plan. Forming a human pyramid, Krishna climbed to the top and reached the butter pots. The gopis, hiding nearby, watched in amazement and amusement as Krishna gleefully ate the butter.

When they finally confronted Him, Krishna, with His innocent smile and captivating eyes, feigned innocence and made excuses that only deepened their enchantment with Him. Unable to stay angry, the gopis found themselves even more charmed by Krishna's divine mischief.

This leela of Mohan underscores Krishna's ability to enchant and captivate through His playful and innocent actions. His butter-stealing episodes brought immense happiness and laughter to the residents of Vrundavan, transforming mundane moments into divine experiences. Krishna, as Mohan, teaches that divinity can be found in the simplicity and joy of everyday life, and that true devotion is characterized by love and delight in the divine presence.

By invoking Krishna as Mohan, devotees seek to experience the enchantment and happiness of His divine presence, recognizing that the divine can transform even the simplest acts into moments of profound spiritual connection and bliss.

36. Murlidhar (Holder of the Flute)

Leela: The Enchanting Melody of Krishna's Flute

Krishna, known as Murlidhar, the holder of the flute, is celebrated for the divine music He creates with His flute. This leela emphasizes Krishna's role as the supreme musician whose melodies enchant and attract all beings, symbolizing the call of the divine to the souls of devotees.

In the idyllic pastures of Vrundavan, Krishna's flute-playing was a source of immense joy and bliss for all who heard it. The melodious sound of Krishna's flute had the power to captivate the hearts of everyone, including the gopis, the cows, and even the inanimate objects like trees and rocks, which would sway and vibrate in response to His divine music.

Krishna's famous leela as Murlidhar is the Rasa Leela, a celestial dance that took place under the full moon on the banks of the Yamuna River. When Krishna played His flute, the divine melody resonated through the hearts of the gopis, who were drawn irresistibly to Him. They left their homes and duties and rushed to the forest to be with Krishna, entranced by the enchanting music.

As the gopis gathered around him, Krishna welcomed them with His charming smile. He then began the Rasa dance, a mystical and divine dance multiplying Himself to be with each gopi. This miraculous feat demonstrated Krishna's ability to be present with each devotee individually, catering to their love and devotion.

This symbolizes the ultimate union between the soul and the divine. Krishna's flute-playing, which initiated the dance, represents the divine call that awakens the soul to its true purpose and draws it towards the divine presence. The gopis' response, characterized by their immediate and unconditional surrender, exemplifies the highest form of bhakti (devotion).

This highlights the importance of divine music as a means of connecting with the divine. The sound of Krishna's flute is not just a physical melody but a spiritual call that transcends the material world and touches the deepest parts of the soul. It teaches that true devotion involves being attuned to the divine call and responding with love and surrender.

By invoking Krishna as Murlidhar, devotees seek to experience the transformative power of His divine music. It signifies the role of music and sound in spiritual practice, illustrating how they can lead to profound states of love, ecstasy, and union with the divine.

37. Muralimanohar (The Enchanter with the Flute)

Leela: Krishna and the Gopis' Yearning

Krishna, known as Muralimanohar, the enchanter with the flute, performed many leelas that demonstrated His ability to captivate and enchant the minds of His devotees with His divine music. One such leela is the episode where Krishna's flute-playing fills the hearts of the gopis with a deep yearning for His presence, illustrating the intense love and longing that characterizes the relationship between the devotee and the divine.

In Vrundavan, the gopis were deeply in love with Krishna, and His absence was always felt intensely by them. Whenever Krishna left the village, the gopis would be consumed by a longing for His return. This longing was most profoundly expressed through the sound of Krishna's flute, which served as a reminder of His divine presence.

One evening, as the gopis were engaged in their daily activities, they heard the distant sound of Krishna's flute. The enchanting melody instantly transported them into a state of divine ecstasy and yearning. Dropping whatever they were doing, the gopis rushed towards the source of the music, their hearts filled with a burning desire to be with Krishna.

As they arrived at the forest where Krishna was playing His flute, they found themselves enveloped in His divine presence. The sound of the flute had created an atmosphere of pure love and bliss, dissolving all their worries and attachments. The gopis, overwhelmed by their love for Krishna, danced and sang in His presence, completely absorbed in the joy of being with Him.

This leela of Muralimanohar emphasizes the power of divine music to evoke deep spiritual emotions and to draw the devotee closer to the divine. The yearning experienced by the gopis represents the soul's longing for union with the divine, a longing that is both painful and blissful.

By invoking Krishna as Muralimanohar, devotees seek to deepen their own sense of longing and love for the divine. This leela teaches that true devotion involves a deep and heartfelt yearning for the divine presence, a yearning that transcends all worldly attachments and leads to spiritual fulfillment.

38. Murari (Enemy of the Selfish and Self-centered people)

Leela: Slaying the Demon Mura

Krishna, known as Murari, the enemy of the demon Mura, is celebrated for His role as the divine protector who vanquishes evil and upholds righteousness. This leela emphasizes Krishna's valor and His commitment to protecting His devotees from malevolent forces.

According to legend, the demon Mura was a formidable asura (demon) who terrorized the heavens and the earth. Empowered by His strength and magical abilities, Mura created havoc, challenging the gods, and spreading fear. In response to the pleas of the gods and sages, Krishna took up the task of confronting and defeating the demon.

In a fierce battle that showcased His supreme strength and divine prowess, Krishna engaged Mura. The demon, confident in his power, used his magical abilities to create illusions and powerful weapons. However, Krishna, with His divine wisdom and skill, countered each of Mura's attacks with ease and precision.

As the battle raged on, Krishna's divine energy and determination overwhelmed the demon. With a decisive strike, Krishna vanquished Mura, restoring peace and order to the universe. This victory demonstrated Krishna's role as the protector of dharma (righteousness) and the vanquisher of evil forces.

The leela of Murari highlights the importance of divine intervention in maintaining cosmic balance and justice. Krishna's defeat of Mura reassures devotees that the divine will always protect them from harm and uphold righteousness. By invoking Krishna as Murari, devotees seek His protection and strength to overcome their own challenges and adversities.

39. Nandgopal (Cowherd of Nanda)

Leela: Saving Cows from Forest-Fire

Krishna, known as Nandgopal, the cowherd of Nanda, is celebrated for His pastoral life in Vrundavan, where He tended to the cows and played with the other cowherd boys. This leela emphasizes Krishna's simple and humble life, highlighting His deep connection with nature and His role as the protector of the cows.

Born to Nanda and Yashoda, Krishna spent His childhood in the idyllic village of Vrundavan. As Nandgopal, Krishna took on the role of a cowherd, spending His days herding cows, playing with His friends, and engaging in various playful and divine pastimes. His presence often gave pleasure to the villagers. His divinity brought prosperity to the village.

Nand gopal
There are several leelas (divine pastimes) that highlight Krishna's role as Gopal, the protector and caretaker of cows. These stories emphasize His deep love for cows and His role as their divine guardian.

One day, while Krishna was taking His cows to the Vrundavan forest with His friends a sudden forest fire swept in, threatening the cows and cowherd boys. On seeing their panic, He calmly swallowed the entire fire to save them all.

This leela speaks of the supreme power of Krishna and how devotedly He protects His devotees and cows, even before extreme danger.

Venu Leela

Every day, Krishna would take the cows to graze in the lush pastures of Vrundavan. To keep the cows calm and happy, Krishna played His flute, mesmerizing not just the cows but also the gopis, birds, trees, and the entire environment. The cows, enchanted by Krishna's divine music, would gather around Him and stop grazing just to listen.

This leela depicts Krishna's loving relationship with the cows and His ability to bring peace and joy to all creatures. His flute symbolizes divine harmony, uniting all beings in bliss.

The Footwear Leela

One day, Krishna, who was still a boy, was about to leave for the forest to graze the cows. Before going out, He saw how harsh and thorny the way would be ahead of Him. He also noticed that the cows would walk barefoot on the hard ground with no protection to their delicate hooves and without any shelter from the sun, stones, and thorns.

Feeling very concerned, Krishna approached His mother, Yashoda, and said: "Mother, you give Me footwear to protect My feet, but what about the cows? Their feet are bare, and they walk such long distances in pain. If they don't have footwear, I cannot wear Mine either!"

Hearing the soothing words, Yashoda smiled and said, "My dear son, how could we possibly make shoes for the thousands and thousands of cows? It would be impossible." Asked Krishna innocently, "If we can't get shoes made for all those cows, I will walk bare feet with them too."

True to His word, Krishna did not wear a single footwear. He walked barefoot with the cows, loved them, and made sure that they were not uncomfortable. This leela added to His more loveable qualities in the minds of the people of Gokul, which saw His immense love and regard for all creation.

This leela showcases the immense compassion of Krishna, even as a child. His concern for the cows reflects His role as their divine protector and as a symbol of ahimsa (non-violence) and care for animals.
Krishna's act of walking barefoot symbolizes His willingness to share the hardships of His devotees. Just as He walked with the cows, He walks with His devotees, sharing their joys and pains.

Though He is the Supreme Lord, Krishna demonstrates humility by putting the comfort of the cows above His own needs. This inspires devotees to cultivate humility and selflessness.

In Vedic traditions, cows are considered sacred and are treated as symbols of motherhood and nourishment. Krishna's love for the cows reinforces their revered status and inspires protection and care for them.

40. Nandakumara (Son of Nanda)

Leela: Krishna's pastimes with Nanda Maharaj

Krishna, known as Nandakumara, the son of Nanda, is celebrated for His delightful and mischievous childhood pastimes in Vrundavan. These leelas highlight the innocence and divine charm of Krishna's early years, endearing Him to His family and the entire village.

As the beloved son of Nanda and Yashoda, Krishna's childhood was filled with playful and miraculous events that showcased His divine nature.

The leelas of Nandakumara emphasize Krishna's divine playfulness, His miraculous abilities, and His role as the beloved child of Nanda and Yashoda. These stories highlight the importance of recognizing the divine in the everyday and finding joy and wonder in the simple moments of life.

By invoking Krishna as Nandakumara, devotees seek to cultivate childlike innocence, joy, and a deep sense of devotion. It shows that the divine is present in every moment, and that true devotion involves seeing the divine in the simple, everyday experiences of life. Krishna, as Nandakumara, embodies the principles of innocence, playfulness, and the profound presence of the divine in the mundane.

Nanda Maharaj, the foster father of Lord Krishna, was a deeply devout and righteous man. He and the people of Vrundavan were completely devoted to Krishna, who was the center of their lives. Despite the presence of the Supreme Lord in their midst, the residents of Vrundavan, including Nanda Maharaj, often experienced events that showed them glimpses of Krishna's divine powers.

The Incident with Varuna Dev

One auspicious day, during the winter season, Nanda Maharaj decided to take an early morning bath in the Yamuna River to perform his daily rituals. He left for the river while it was still dark, before the break of dawn, not realizing that it was the time when Varuna, the god of the waters, held dominion over the river.

As Nanda Maharaj entered the waters to bathe, the servants of Varuna Dev noticed him. Mistaking Nanda Maharaj's early entry into the river as a violation of their lord's time, they captured him and took him to Varuna Dev's underwater palace.

When the people of Vrundavan realized that Nanda Maharaj was missing, they were filled with fear and anxiety. They immediately rushed to Krishna, who was still a young boy at the time, and informed Him of the situation. Knowing that Krishna was no ordinary child, they implored Him to save His father.

Krishna, ever the protector of His devotees, smiled reassuringly and immediately set off for the underwater kingdom of Varuna. As He entered Varuna's domain, the god of the waters was astonished to see Krishna. He immediately realized that Krishna was none other than the Supreme Personality of Godhead, whom he worshipped with great reverence.

Varuna Dev fell at Krishna's feet and begged for forgiveness, explaining that his servants had made a mistake in capturing Nanda Maharaj. He praised Krishna's divine pastimes and expressed his gratitude for the opportunity to witness his Lord's form.

Krishna, always merciful, accepted Varuna Dev's apology. He then asked for the safe return of Nanda Maharaj. Varuna Dev happily complied, and Nanda Maharaj was brought back to Vrundavan unharmed.

When Nanda Maharaj safely returned to the surface, he was both relieved and awestruck by the events that had transpired. He had been taken to an otherworldly realm, but Krishna had come to his rescue, further solidifying his faith in his son's divine nature.

Upon his return, Nanda Maharaj shared his experience with the other residents of Vrundavan. They were amazed by Krishna's divine intervention and began to realize more deeply that Krishna was indeed the Supreme Lord, though He lived among them as a simple cowherd boy.

This leela underscores the divine protection Krishna provides to His devotees. Nanda Maharaj's abduction by Varuna Dev and His subsequent rescue by Krishna illustrate Krishna's omnipresence and His commitment to ensuring the safety of those who love and worship Him. It also serves to remind the devotees of Krishna's divine nature, showing that even gods like Varuna are in awe of Him and seek His mercy.

The story also deepens the relationship between Krishna and the residents of Vrundavan, especially His father, Nanda Maharaj. It reassures them that Krishna, though appearing as their beloved son and friend, can overcome any obstacle to protect and care for them, further nurturing their unwavering devotion.

Krishna Holding Nanda Maharaj's Footwear

In the simple and beautiful village of Vrundavan, Krishna was known not just for His divine powers but also for His immense love and devotion to His parents, particularly His foster father, Nanda Maharaj. One day, when Nanda Maharaj had to leave home to attend to some important work, a sweet and touching incident occurred that has become one of the most endearing leelas of Krishna's childhood.

Nanda Maharaj had left his footwear outside the house before entering, as was customary. When he was about to leave, Krishna, who was still a little boy, noticed His father preparing to go out. Wanting to help, Krishna quickly picked up His father's footwear.

With great enthusiasm and love, Krishna placed the sandals on His head and walked towards Nanda Maharaj. Despite being the Supreme Personality of Godhead, Krishna, in His childlike form, did not hesitate to perform this humble act. He carried the sandals with such care and devotion, smiling all the while, as He approached His father.

Nanda Maharaj was deeply moved by this gesture. Seeing his little son, who was none other than the protector of the universe, carrying his sandals on his head, filled Nanda Maharaj's heart with overwhelming love and affection. He gently took the sandals from Krishna and embraced Him with tears of joy and pride.

The sight of Krishna performing such a humble service out of pure love for His father left an indelible mark on the hearts of the residents of Vrundavan. They marveled at the way Krishna, despite being divine, found joy in serving his parents and elders with utmost sincerity.

This leela is a profound demonstration of Krishna's humility and devotion to his parents. Despite being the Supreme Lord, Krishna showed that true love and respect are expressed through service, no matter how simple or humble the task may be.

For devotees, this leela is a reminder of the importance of serving one's parents and elders with love and humility. Krishna's act of carrying Nanda Maharaj's sandals on his head exemplifies how even the smallest acts of service, when performed with devotion, can be expressions of the highest love.

Furthermore, this leela highlights the principle that in the eyes of true love, no service is too small or beneath one's dignity. Krishna's actions teach us that divine love is shown through the willingness to serve others selflessly, regardless of one's status or position.

This charming incident from Krishna's childhood continues to inspire devotees to emulate His humility and love in their own lives, encouraging them to honor and serve their parents and elders with the same devotion that Krishna showed towards Nanda Maharaj.

41. Narayan (The Supreme Being)

Leela: The Universal Form in the Bhagavad Gita

The name Narayana means "the one who rests on water" (from nara, meaning water, and ayana, meaning resting place). This imagery is symbolic of the cosmic waters from which the universe is said to emerge, with Narayana as the eternal source. Krishna, as the manifestation of Narayana, is seen as the eternal, all-pervading source from which all creation flows, embodying the infinite nature of Narayana.

In many Hindu scriptures, particularly the Puranas and the Mahabharata, Krishna is addressed as Narayana by sages, devotees, and other divine beings, emphasizing His supreme status. For example, during the Kurukshetra war, Bhishma, one of the greatest warriors, refers to Krishna as Narayana, recognizing His divine and supreme nature.

Krishna, known as Narayan, the Supreme Being, is often depicted as the source of all creation and the ultimate reality. One of the most significant leelas that highlight Krishna's identity as Narayan is His revelation of the Universal Form (Vishvarupa) to Arjuna in the Bhagavad Gita.

Krishna is called Narayana because in Hindu theology, Krishna is understood to be a full manifestation of Narayana, who is the Supreme Being and source of all creation in Vaishnavism. The name Narayana has several meanings, and it is commonly associated with the Supreme Lord Vishnu, who is also identified with Krishna in many scriptures.

In the Bhagavad Gita, Krishna reveals to Arjuna that He is the Supreme Being, the original source of everything. Narayana is another name for this Supreme Being, emphasizing His eternal nature and omnipresence. As Krishna declares His divinity and His identity as the ultimate cause of all that exists, it becomes clear that Krishna and Narayana are one and the same.

Narayana is often depicted as the protector of the universe, residing in the cosmic ocean, from which all creation emerges. Krishna, in His many leelas, takes on this role of protector, particularly when He incarnates on Earth to destroy evil and uphold dharma (righteousness). His acts of saving devotees, vanquishing demons, and restoring cosmic order align Him with the characteristics of Narayana.

In texts like the Srimad Bhagavatam and Mahabharata, Krishna is consistently referred to as Narayana or the Supreme Being who takes various forms to protect the universe.

Krishna is called Narayana because He embodies all the divine qualities, attributes, and roles associated with Narayana, the

Supreme Being in Vaishnavism. This identification underscores Krishna's role as the ultimate protector, creator, and sustainer of the universe, making him synonymous with Narayana in the Hindu tradition.

42. Navanitchor/ Makhanchor (The Butter Thief)

Leela: Krishna's Butter Stealing Episodes

Krishna, known as Navanitchor, the butter thief, is celebrated for His mischievous and endearing childhood activities, particularly His love for stealing butter from the homes of the gopis in Vrundavan. This leela highlights Krishna's playful nature and His ability to endear Himself to His devotees through His charming antics.

As a young child, Krishna's fondness for butter led Him to devise numerous clever ways to steal it. Despite their efforts to hide the butter in high places or secure pots, the gopis found themselves unable to keep it away from Krishna's mischievous grasp. His friends often joined Him, creating an adventurous game out of their butter-stealing exploits.

One day, the gopis, tired of Krishna's constant thefts, decided to catch Him red-handed. They formed a plan and hid themselves while leaving the butter in an accessible place. Krishna, unaware of their scheme, arrived with His friends and began relishing the butter. Just as they were about to enjoy their spoils, the gopis jumped out and caught them.

Krishna, with His innocent and captivating smile, feigned innocence, claiming He was only there to protect the butter from being stolen by others. The gopis, despite their initial annoyance, found themselves enchanted by Krishna's charm and wit, unable to stay angry with him for long.

In Damodar leela, (which has been discussed earlier) Yashoda, Krishna's mother, decided to tie Him up as a punishment for His incessant mischief. Using a rope, she attempted to bind Krishna to a mortar, but no matter how many ropes she added, they always fell short by a tiny length. Realizing Her son's divine nature, Yashoda's frustration turned to awe and devotion, and she ultimately embraced Krishna, overwhelmed by His divinity and love.

The leela of Navanitchor illustrates the intimate and playful relationship between Krishna and His devotees. His butter-stealing episodes, while mischievous, brought immense joy and love to the hearts of the gopis and the residents of Vrundavan.

43. Nirguna (Beyond All Attributes)

Leela: Krishna's Formless Guidance to Uddhava

Krishna, known as Nirguna, the one beyond all attributes, is celebrated for His transcendental nature, which transcends material qualities and dualities. This leela is best illustrated in Krishna's guidance to His devotee Uddhava, as described in the Uddhava Gita, a part of the Srimad Bhagavatam.

Towards the end of His earthly presence, Krishna decided to impart final teachings to His dear friend and devotee, Uddhava. Uddhava was deeply distressed by the impending departure of Krishna from the material world and sought guidance on how to live and attain spiritual liberation in Krishna's absence. In their profound conversation, Krishna revealed the principles of Nirguna Bhakti, or devotion to the formless, attribute less Supreme Being. Krishna explained that while He manifests in various forms to interact with His devotees, His ultimate nature is beyond any material attributes or limitations. He is the unchanging, formless essence that pervades all existence.

Krishna taught Uddhava that true devotion transcends the worship of His physical form and focuses on realizing His Nirguna aspect. This form of devotion involves recognizing the divine presence in everything and understanding the underlying unity of all creation. Krishna emphasized the importance of meditating on the formless aspect of the divine, cultivating detachment from material desires, and developing unwavering devotion.

In one instance, Krishna narrated the story of the Avadhuta, a sage who learned spiritual lessons from observing nature and living beings. The Avadhuta's realization of the Nirguna Brahman—Krishna's formless aspect—illustrated how one could attain wisdom and liberation by perceiving the divine beyond physical appearances and attributes.

Krishna's teachings to Uddhava on Nirguna Bhakti highlight the importance of transcending superficial forms and attributes to connect with the eternal, unmanifested essence of the divine. By focusing on the Nirguna aspect, devotees can achieve a deeper, more profound spiritual realization.

This leela underscores that while Krishna manifests in various forms to engage with His devotees, His ultimate nature is formless and beyond material qualities. By invoking Krishna as Nirguna, devotees are reminded to look beyond the physical and material aspects of life and seek the eternal, unchanging divine presence within and around them.

44. Parabrahmana (The Supreme Absolute Truth)

Leela: Krishna's Revelation to Brahma

Krishna, known as Parabrahmana, the Supreme Absolute Truth, is the ultimate reality that encompasses and transcends all that exists. This leela is beautifully illustrated in the Brahma-Vimohana Leela, where Krishna reveals His supreme nature to Lord Brahma. One day, the creator god Brahma decided to test the divinity of young Krishna, who was playing with His cowherd friends and calves in Vrundavan. Brahma used His mystic powers to hide the calves and the boys, thinking that Krishna, if He was truly divine, would find a way to handle the situation.

Unperturbed, Krishna, who is the Parabrahmana, manifested identical forms of the missing boys and calves, continuing the daily activities as if nothing had happened. Each of these forms was a complete and perfect replica, indistinguishable from the originals, and displayed the same divine qualities as Krishna Himself.

After a year in the celestial realm, Brahma returned to see how His test had fared. To His astonishment, He saw the cowherd boys and calves exactly as He had left them, playing happily

with Krishna. Confused and humbled, Brahma realized the enormity of Krishna's divine power.
At that moment, Krishna dispelled the illusion, revealing His true form as the Parabrahmana. Brahma saw countless universes emanating from Krishna's body, each containing myriad forms of creation, preservation, and destruction. He understood that Krishna is the source of all existence, the Supreme Absolute Truth beyond comprehension.

Overwhelmed with awe and devotion, Brahma bowed down to Krishna, acknowledging His supreme nature, and seeking forgiveness for His pride and ignorance. Krishna, ever compassionate, accepted Brahma's repentance, and restored the original calves and cowherd boys.

This leela of Parabrahmana underscores Krishna's position as the ultimate reality and the source of all creation. It highlights the futility of trying to comprehend the divine through limited human understanding and emphasizes the importance of humility and devotion.

By invoking Krishna as Parabrahmana, devotees are reminded of the vastness and incomprehensibility of the divine. This leela teaches that true wisdom lies in recognizing the supreme nature of Krishna and surrendering to His divine will with humility and reverence.

45. Paramatma (The Supersoul)

Leela: Krishna's Presence in the Heart

Krishna, known as Paramatma, the Supersoul, is the indwelling presence within the hearts of all living beings. This leela is exemplified in the story of Krishna and the sage Narada, which illustrates how Krishna manifests as the inner guide and witness in every being.

The great sage Narada, curious about Krishna's all-pervasive nature, once asked Him how He could reside simultaneously in the hearts of all beings. Krishna, understanding Narada's curiosity, decided to demonstrate His omnipresence as Paramatma.

Krishna invited Narada to accompany Him to a series of different households. At each place, Krishna was already present in the hearts of the residents, guiding and witnessing their actions. Whether it was a devout Brahmin engaged in rituals, a farmer tilling his land, or a housewife attending to her chores, Krishna was present in each heart, fulfilling His role as the Paramatma.

Narada, observing this divine play, realized that Krishna, as the Paramatma, was indeed present within every individual, regardless of their activities or consciousness. Krishna explained that as the Supersoul, He resides in the heart of every being, guiding them from within, witnessing their actions, and providing inspiration and support.

This leela of Paramatma highlights the intimate and personal relationship between the divine and every living being. Krishna, as the Supersoul, is always present within, offering guidance, support, and witnessing the soul's journey.

By invoking Krishna as Paramatma, devotees seek to connect with the divine presence within their own hearts. This leela teaches that the divine is always with us, guiding us from within, and that true spiritual realization involves recognizing and communing with the Supersoul.

46. Parampurusha (The Supreme Person)

Leela: Krishna's Pastimes in Vrundavan

Krishna, known as Parampurusha, the Supreme Person, embodies the highest ideals of divine personality, combining the attributes of supreme power, beauty, wisdom, and compassion. This leela is best illustrated through Krishna's pastimes in Vrundavan, where He displayed His divine qualities and engaged intimately with His devotees.

By invoking Krishna as Parampurusha, devotees seek to experience the fullness of His divine personality. This leela teaches that the supreme person is not only all-powerful and all-knowing but also deeply compassionate and loving, always ready to protect and uplift his devotees.

47. Patitapavan/ Karunanidhi/Dina Bandhu/Bhaktvatsala

(Redeemer of the Fallen, an ocean of Compassion)
Leela- The Flattened rice

One of the most touching episodes in Krishna's life is the leela of Krishna and Sudama, depicting His humility, friendship, and generosity. This leela has made names like Sakha (friend), Bhaktavatsala (one who loves His devotees), and Dina Bandhu (friend of the poor) synonymous with Krishna.

Sudama, also known as Kuchela in South Indian traditions, was a childhood friend and classmate of Krishna at the ashram of Guru Sandipani. While Krishna became a king, Sudama lived a life of poverty as a humble Brahmin. Despite his hardships, Sudama was deeply devoted to Krishna and held no complaints about his condition.

Encouraged by his wife, Sudama went to Krishna in Dwaraka to seek His help though he was very hesitant due to his humility. He carried with him a small bundle of poha (flattened rice) as all that he could carry.

Krishna welcomed Sudama with open arms and, washing his feet, embracing him, and giving him the seat of honor, made him feel comfortable. Rukmini, among the other queens, respectfully served Sudama.

Due to Sudama's reluctance, Krishna lovingly took the poha and enjoyed it with great pleasure, declaring that it was the most precious gift He ever received. It had never occurred to Krishna to expect help from Sudama. When Sudama returned home, he found that his humble hut had become a palace and his family was showered with prosperity.

There is spiritual significance in the Leela, which is true devotion.

Krishna values love and devotion more than material wealth. Sudama's offering of simple poha was more valuable to Him than gold or jewels.

Krishna does not wait for His devotees to ask for help. He knows their needs and fulfills them out of His boundless grace.

The leela shows that Krishna sees no distinction between rich and poor. His love is equally accessible to all who approach Him with a pure heart.

48. Ranchod (One Who Ran Away from The Battlefield)

Leela: Killing of Kalayavan by Muchukunda

Ranchod is a name of Krishna that means "the one who fled the battlefield." This name highlights Krishna's strategic wisdom in choosing to avoid unnecessary conflict to achieve a higher purpose.

During one of His battles, Krishna faced the mighty demon Kalayavan, who was invincible and had obtained a boon making him undefeatable in combat. Krishna, recognizing that direct confrontation would be unwise, led Kalayavan into a cave where the ancient king Muchukunda was sleeping.

Muchukunda had been granted a boon by the gods that whoever disturbed his sleep would be reduced to ashes by his gaze. Krishna, knowing this, entered the cave and used His divine power to awaken Muchukunda just as Kalayavan followed him inside.

As Kalayavan entered the cave, he mistook the sleeping Muchukunda for Krishna and kicked him, waking the king. Muchukunda opened his eyes, and the fiery power of his gaze instantly turned Kalayavan to ashes, thus eliminating the threat.

This leela demonstrates Krishna's strategic wisdom and His ability to use non-violent means to achieve victory, thereby earning the name Ranchod. By leading Kalayavan to his doom through cleverness rather than direct combat, Krishna avoided unnecessary bloodshed and demonstrated the importance of using intellect and strategy over brute force.

Devotees learn from this leela the value of strategic thinking and the power of divine wisdom. Krishna's actions as Ranchod show that sometimes, avoiding confrontation and using intelligence is a greater form of strength. It reassures devotees that Krishna protects them through His divine wisdom, often in ways that are not immediately apparent. This story encourages them to trust in Krishna's plans and to seek non-violent, intelligent solutions in their own lives, reinforcing faith in Krishna's protective and all-knowing nature.

49. Shyam (The Dark blue, black)

Leela: Krishna's Youthful Charm and Beauty

Krishna, known as Shyam, embodies the captivating dark complexion that enhances his divine charm and beauty. This leela focuses on Krishna's youthful exploits in Vrundavan, where his dark complexion became a source of attraction and admiration among the residents, especially the gopis.

From an early age, Krishna's enchanting appearance and charismatic personality drew people towards Him. His dark complexion, resembling a rain-filled cloud, added to His allure, earning him the endearing epithet "Shyam."

Krishna's dark complexion symbolizes the infinite depths of His divine nature. It represents the mystery and profundity of the Supreme Being, drawing devotees into deeper contemplation and adoration.

By invoking Krishna as Shyam, devotees are reminded of His captivating beauty and the irresistible charm that attracts all beings towards Him. This leela teaches that Krishna's dark complexion symbolizes the all-encompassing nature of divine love, drawing devotees into a profound spiritual journey towards union with the Supreme.

50. Shyamsundar (One who resembles the beauty of evening)

Leela: Krishna's Childhood and Youthful Exploits

Krishna, known as Shyamsundar, embodies the enchanting beauty and charm of His dark complexion during His childhood and youthful exploits. This leela focuses on Krishna's playful and mischievous activities in Vrundavan and His endearing interactions with the residents, especially the cowherd boys and girls.

As Shyamsundar, Krishna's childhood is filled with delightful leelas that highlight His divine nature and His intimate relationship with His devotees. His leelas like the stealing of butter or Yashoda trying to tie Him with a rope or even the lifting of the Govardhan hill demonstrates Krishna's playful nature as Shyamsundar and His affectionate relationship with Yashoda, Nand and all His devotees.

Shyamsundar's divine beauty and charm attract not only the residents of Vrundavan but also devotees across the world who are drawn to Krishna's playful and loving nature. His interactions with the gopis and cowherd boys exemplify the deep bond of love and trust that exists between the devotee and the divine.

By invoking Krishna as Shyamsundar, devotees seek to experience the joy and innocence of His childhood and youthful adventures. This leela teaches that Krishna's enchanting beauty and divine charm inspire devotion and love, drawing devotees closer to Him in Their spiritual journey.

51.Vasudeva (son of Vasudeva)

Leela: Vasudeva carrying baby Krishna

Vasudeva is another name for Krishna, meaning "son of Vasudeva." It highlights Krishna's divine birth in the prison of King Kamsa. Vasudeva, Krishna's father, carried baby Krishna across the Yamuna river to Gokul to save him from Kamsa's wrath.

The story of Vasudeva carrying baby Krishna across the Yamuna river amidst a storm. The river Yamuna parted herself to allow their passage. This is a powerful example of divine intervention. It illustrates that when one has unwavering faith and trust in the divine, miraculous protection and guidance are always available. This is an inspiration for the devotees to remain steadfast and courageous in the face of life's challenges.

This leela encourages them to face challenges with courage and faith, knowing that Krishna is always with them, guiding and protecting them through difficult times.

Vasudeva represents the divine faith and miraculous nature of Krishna's birth. This name emphasizes Krishna's role as a savior and protector from evil. It also reflects the faith and devotion of Vasudeva and Devaki.

52. Vithal or Vithoba (Gives Fortune)

Leela: Krishna waiting for the darshan of His devotee Pundalik

Vithoba, a form of Krishna, is worshiped predominantly in Maharashtra. According to legend, Krishna appeared as Vithoba to His devotee Pundalik, standing on a brick with hands on hips, waiting for Pundalik's darshan. This form shows Krishna's humility and love for his devotees.

The story of Vithoba and Pundalik revolves around the devoted son, Pundalik, who was dedicated to serving his elderly parents. Despite Krishna's appearance at his doorstep, Pundalik prioritized his parents, asking Krishna to wait by standing on a brick. Impressed by His devotion and humility, Krishna patiently waited, embodying the form of Vithoba.

This leela teaches the profound values of serving one's parents and being selflessly devoted to duty. The pilgrimage to Pandharpur, where Vithoba is worshipped, brings devotees together, strengthening their faith and devotion, and fostering a deep sense of spiritual community and shared purpose.

Vithoba signifies the close relationship between Krishna and His devotees. The deity's posture, waiting patiently, highlights His compassion and willingness to be present for His devotees. Vithoba's temple in Pandharpur is a major pilgrimage site.

53. Vishwaroopa (The form of the Universe)

Leela: Showing of the Universe to Mother Yashoda in his little mouth

When Yashoda saw the universe within Krishna's mouth, she referred to him as "Vishwaroopa," which means "the form of the universe." This name reflects the divine and all-encompassing nature of Krishna.

The Universe in Krishna's Mouth

One day, while playing with His friends, little Krishna was accused of eating mud. His friends complained to his mother, Yashoda, who, concerned for His well-being, scolded Krishna and asked Him to open His mouth. Reluctantly, Krishna opened His mouth to prove His innocence. To Yashoda's astonishment, instead of finding mud, she saw the entire universe within His mouth.

Inside Krishna's mouth, Yashoda witnessed the vast expanse of creation: galaxies, stars, planets, the earth, and all living beings. She saw rivers, mountains, oceans, and all the elements of the cosmos. She even saw herself, holding Krishna, in His mouth. This divine vision overwhelmed her, revealing the true, infinite nature of her child. Yashoda was momentarily stunned and awestruck by this miraculous sight.

Overwhelmed by the enormity and divinity of what she had seen, Yashoda experienced a mixture of awe and fear. She could not comprehend the full extent of Krishna's divine nature. To comfort her and restore her maternal affection, Krishna used His divine power to make her forget the vision. Yashoda once again saw Him as her mischievous, beloved son, and the memory of the cosmic vision faded.

This leela highlights the paradoxical nature of Krishna's divine incarnation. He is simultaneously the innocent, playful child and the supreme, all-encompassing deity who holds the entire universe within Himself. For devotees, this story emphasizes Krishna's boundless power and His ability to manifest the divine in the most intimate, everyday moments.

The leela of Vishwaroopa serves as a reminder of the omnipresence of the divine in all aspects of life. It inspires devotees to recognize the sacred in the mundane and to approach life with reverence and humility, knowing that the divine is present in all things, even in the playful antics of a child.

54. Yashodanandan (Son of Yashoda)

Leela: Krishna's Bond with Mother Yashoda

Krishna, known as Yashodanandan, is celebrated for His deep and loving relationship with His mother, Yashoda. This leela focuses on Krishna's childhood in Vrundavan and His endearing interactions with Yashoda, highlighting their bond of motherly affection and divine love.

Yashoda, the wife of Nanda Maharaj, was blessed with Krishna as her son, whom she loved dearly and cared for with utmost devotion. Despite Krishna's divine nature, Yashoda treated Him as her beloved child, nourishing Him, playing with Him, and showering Him with affection.

Krishna, known as Yashodanandan, shared a profound and affectionate relationship with His mother, Yashoda.

One endearing leela is when Krishna, as a child, would steal butter from the neighbors' homes, earning the nickname "Makhan Chor" (butter thief).

Despite Yashoda's attempts to discipline him, she was charmed by his mischievous antics.

In another leela, Yashoda would lovingly bathe and dress Krishna, adorning him with beautiful clothes and ornaments.

Her deep maternal love exemplifies the divine bond between them, where the infinite Supreme Being is cherished as a simple, playful child.

55. Yogeshwar (One Who Teaches Yoga)

Leela: Krishna's Teachings on Yoga in the Bhagavad Gita

Krishna, known as Yogeshwar, is celebrated for His profound teachings on yoga and spirituality, as elucidated in the Bhagavad Gita. This leela focuses on Krishna's role as the supreme master of yoga, guiding Arjuna and humanity towards spiritual enlightenment and self-realization.

Krishna, as Yogeshwar, also elucidates the concept of Bhakti-yoga, the path of loving devotion to the divine. He explains that devotion offered with pure love and sincerity is the most effective means to attain union with the Supreme. Krishna encourages Arjuna to surrender to him completely, offering all actions and thoughts in devotion and trust.

During the Kurukshetra war, Arjuna, overwhelmed by moral dilemmas and the impending battle, turned to Krishna for guidance. In response, Krishna imparted timeless wisdom through the Bhagavad Gita, addressing Arjuna's doubts and teaching him the path of righteousness, devotion, and selfless action.

Krishna's teachings as Yogeshwar encompass various forms of yoga, including karma yoga (the yoga of selfless action), bhakti yoga (the yoga of devotion), and jnana yoga (the yoga of knowledge). He explains that true yoga is not just physical exercises but a holistic approach to life that integrates spiritual principles into every aspect of existence.

One of the pivotal teachings of Yogeshwar Krishna is the concept of Stitha-prajna, the steadfast consciousness. Krishna describes the qualities of a true yogi who remains equipoised amidst joy and sorrow, success and failure, honor and dishonor. Such a yogi, Krishna explains, is detached from material desires and is focused on spiritual realization.

Another significant teaching is Dhyana-yoga, the yoga of meditation. Krishna instructs Arjuna to fix His mind on Him and engage in uninterrupted devotion. He emphasizes the importance of controlling the mind and senses through regular practice and detachment from worldly distractions. By focusing the mind on Krishna, the supreme object of meditation, one can attain spiritual liberation and realize the true self.

In the Vibhuti-yoga chapter, Krishna reveals His divine glories and manifestations, demonstrating His omnipresence and omnipotence. He explains that every aspect of creation is a manifestation of His divine energy and presence. By contemplating these divine manifestations, one can develop reverence and devotion towards the Supreme.

Krishna's teachings as Yogeshwar are comprehensive and timeless, offering practical guidance on how to lead a meaningful and spiritual life. He teaches Arjuna—and through him, all humanity—the principles of righteous action (dharma), devotion (bhakti), and knowledge (jnana) that lead to spiritual fulfillment and liberation.

Yogeshwar Krishna's discourse in the Bhagavad Gita transcends the battlefield of Kurukshetra, becoming a universal scripture that continues to inspire and guide people from all walks of life. His teachings emphasize the importance of inner purity, selfless service, and unwavering devotion as essential components of the path to self-realization.

Devotees invoke Krishna as Yogeshwar to seek guidance and inspiration in their spiritual journey. By following His teachings on yoga and spirituality, devotees strive to attain inner peace, wisdom, and ultimately, union with the Supreme.

B: Krishna's Names with Radha and Related Leelas

The names of Radha and Krishna together evoke the purest form of divine love, unity, and spiritual connection. Taking the names of Radha and Krishna together holds deep spiritual significance. Radha represents supreme devotion and love, while Krishna embodies the divine, the object of that love. Together, Their names symbolize the union of the soul with the Divine, emphasizing that pure love and devotion are the paths to attaining the ultimate spiritual connection. Chanting "Radha-Krishna" invokes both the qualities of divine love and the joy of the beloved's presence, bringing about a sense of inner peace, spiritual upliftment, and a reminder of the eternal, blissful bond between the devotee and the Divine.

1. Radha Damodar (The bounded Lord)

Leela-Bounded by Radha's Love

The name "Damodar" itself holds a deep meaning. It is derived from two Sanskrit words: "dama," meaning rope, and "udara," meaning belly. Traditionally, it refers to the pastime where Mother Yashoda binds young Krishna to a grinding mortar with a rope, symbolizing His submission to pure love. However, when we add "Radha" to this name, it transforms the meaning into something even more profound, emphasizing Krishna's willingness to be bound not just by Yashoda's motherly love but by Radha's divine love and devotion.

The Kunja Leela

One day during the sacred month of Kartika, Krishna, also known as Shyama, arrived late for a meeting with Radha in Her private garden, or kunja. Radha, feeling hurt and upset, looked at Him with loving anger and tied a golden vine around Krishna's waist, wanting to teach Him a lesson for not keeping His promise. Krishna, pleading with Radha, explained that He was late because His mother, Yashoda, had kept Him home for a festival. Realizing her mistake, Radha quickly untied Him, and Their love deepened. The Vrajavasis (residents of Vrundavan) adore Krishna even more as Damodara, the one bound by Radha's love

Beyond the story where Radha ties Krishna with a golden vine, another significant pastime reflects the loving relationship between Radha and Damodar. It is said that once, Radha was eagerly waiting for Krishna in the kunja, but He was late. Radha, with tears of both longing and mild frustration, decided to create a beautiful garland of wildflowers to present to Him. When Krishna finally arrived, Radha, still slightly upset, wrapped the garland around Krishna's neck, but instead of just adorning Him, the garland miraculously turned into a glowing rope that bound Krishna. This rope, however, did not restrict Him physically but symbolized the eternal bond of love and devotion that Radha held over Krishna's heart. Seeing Krishna smile, Radha's own heart melted, and the garland returned to its original form, signifying the harmony between them.

The Venu Leela

In another leela, Krishna, known for playing the flute (venu), once teased Radha by playing a tune that enchanted the gopis, drawing them towards Him, but He deliberately avoided Radha's gaze. Radha, feeling a mix of longing and playful anger, decided to take Krishna's flute from Him. In Her divine mood, She proclaimed that until Krishna played a tune dedicated only to Her, He would not get His flute back. Krishna, enjoying the playful interaction, pretended to resist but eventually agreed. He then played a melody so sweet, focusing solely on Radha, that even the birds and trees seemed to sway to its tune. Overwhelmed by the pure devotion expressed through the music, Radha returned the flute to Krishna, and in that moment, Krishna, moved by Her love, declared that She had bound Him with Her affection, further solidifying His identity as Damodar.

The story of Radha Damodar is a name that signifies the deep and eternal bond between Radha and Krishna. This bond is not just one of affection but of divine love and devotion, where even the Supreme Being, Krishna, willingly allows Himself to be bound by the love of His dearest beloved, Radha. The stories associated with this name reveal the profound sweetness and intimacy of their relationship, making Radha Damodar a cherished name in the hearts of devotees.

It is a reminder to devotees that the pure, selfless love that Radha embodies is so powerful that it can bind even the infinite, all-powerful Krishna. This divine love is what makes Radha Damodar a name that resonates deeply within the hearts of all who seek to understand the true nature of divine love and devotion.

2. Radhe Eshwar (The Lord of Radha)

Leela-The Flower Garden

In the enchanting atmosphere of Vrundavan, where every tree and plant seemed to sway in rhythm with the divine love of Radha and Krishna, the garden served as a sacred haven for Their secret meetings. This garden, nestled in the heart of Vrundavan. It was not just any ordinary place; it was a celestial abode where the essence of Their love blossomed with every petal and fragrance that filled the air. The flowers, vibrant and diverse, seemed to compete with one another to catch a glimpse of this divine couple, their colors glowing even brighter in the presence of such pure love.

Krishna, known for His playful and mischievous nature, teased Radha a little too much, causing Her to feel upset. She turned Her face away from Him, Her heart heavy with a mix of love and indignation. The garden, which usually echoed with Their laughter and sweet exchanges, suddenly felt silent and still, as if sharing Radha's mood. Krishna, observing the change in Radha's demeanor, felt a pang of regret. He knew that Her love for Him was unparalleled, and the thought of causing Her even the slightest discomfort troubled Him deeply.

Determined to win back Her smile, Krishna began to gather flowers from the garden. But these were not just any flowers;

each one was carefully chosen for its unique beauty and fragrance, each one symbolizing a different aspect of their divine relationship. As He wove the garland, the flowers seemed to come alive in His hands, their scents blending into a heavenly aroma that filled the garden. The garland was more than just a collection of flowers—it was a token of His deep and sincere love for Radha, a silent apology, and a promise to cherish her forever.

When Krishna approached Radha with the garland, His eyes reflected a mixture of love, playfulness, and earnestness. Without saying a word, He placed the garland around Her neck, letting His actions speak for His feelings. The touch of the flowers, combined with the warmth of Krishna's love, melted away Radha's anger. She felt the depth of His affection and realized that behind all His playful antics was a heart that beat only for Her.

As Radha looked into Krishna's eyes, She saw not just a mischievous lover but the embodiment of divine love itself. Her heart softened, and a gentle smile graced Her lips. The garden, which had been holding its breath, seemed to come alive again, with birds chirping melodiously and the trees swaying gently as if celebrating the reconciliation of the divine couple.

The rest of the day was spent in the bliss of each other's company. They wandered through the garden, hand in hand, sharing laughter, sweet whispers, and moments of profound silence that spoke volumes. The flowers that adorned the garland seemed to glow brighter as they basked in the couple's divine aura. Every corner of the garden witnessed their love, and even the smallest of creatures felt blessed to be in their presence.

This leela beautifully illustrates the Madhurya Ras, or the sweet and intimate nature of Radha and Krishna's relationship. It showcases Krishna's role not just as a mischievous lover but as a caring and devoted partner who goes to great lengths to ensure Radha's happiness. The act of creating and presenting the garland symbolizes Krishna's acknowledgment of Radha's feelings and His commitment to nurturing their divine bond. The tender moments of reconciliation highlight the depth of their love, making this leela a poignant reminder of the inseparable connection between Radha and Krishna, a bond that is celebrated and revered by devotees across the world.

3. Radha Gopinath (Lord of the gopis)

Leela-The Eternal Bond With Radha and Gopis

The name "Radha Gopinath" highlights the eternal bond between Radha and Krishna, where Krishna is adored as "Gopinath," the Lord of the gopis (cowherd maidens) and Radha is His beloved. This name evokes the divine love and playful pastimes (leelas) between Radha and Krishna, especially in the enchanting land of Vrundavan.

One such leela that beautifully illustrates this bond is the "Raas Leela," where Krishna, as Gopinath, danced with Radha and the gopis on the banks of the Yamuna River on a full moon night. The Raas Leela is the pinnacle of divine love, where Krishna multiplied Himself to dance with each gopi, yet His heart remained with Radha, His supreme beloved. In this divine dance, every gopi felt Krishna's presence with her, but Radha's love was so powerful that Krishna could not keep His attention away from Her.

In one moment during the Raas, Krishna, wanting to emphasize Radha's unparalleled love and devotion, disappeared from the scene along with Radha, leaving the other gopis searching for Him. The gopis wandered through the forests, calling out to Krishna, asking the trees, plants, and animals if they had seen their beloved Gopinath. After sometime, Krishna left Radha and disappeared in the forest. Radha, feeling Krishna's absence, also experienced the intense pain of separation, which only deepened Her love.

Realizing the deep love Radha had for Him, Krishna returned to Her, and They shared a private, intimate moment. But knowing the importance of all the gopis' devotion, Krishna eventually returned to the group, and the Raas Leela resumed, with Radha by His side.

The Rasa Leela, one of the most cherished leela of the divine couple has already been discussed earlier. The dance that took place on a full moon night on the banks of the Yamuna River, symbolizes the soul's desire to merge with the divine. Here Krishna represents the supreme consciousness and Radha the individual soul or bhakti (devotion). Their union in the dance signified the ultimate goal of spiritual life—union with the divine.

This leela of Radha Gopinath not only highlights the deep, unconditional love between Radha and Krishna but also serves as a metaphor for the soul's eternal quest for union with the Divine. Devotees see this pastime as an expression of the highest form of spiritual love, where the soul (Radha) seeks and rejoices in the presence of the Divine (Gopinath). It teaches that true love is selfless, pure, and focused solely on the beloved, mirroring the relationship between Radha and Gopinath.

4. Radha Govind (The Protector of Cows, Devotees and Dharm)

Leela- Divine Love in the Forest of Vrundavan

Krishna is called Radha Govind because He is the eternal consort of Radha and the protector of cows, devotees, and dharma.

Govind is the synonym for many:

Go as in cows; or as our senses, meaning the earth: vind means to provide nourishment/love and cherishing.

When combined with Radha, Radha Govind denotes Krishna as the beloved of Radha, who rules and meets all Her wants with divine love.

One of the most enchanting leelas associated with the name Radha Govind takes place in the forests of Vrundavan. Krishna, surrounded by the gopis and cowherd boys, often played the flute to call the cows. However, when He played a special melody, it would specifically attract Radha, who was the supreme embodiment of love and devotion.

In this particular leela, Krishna was grazing the cows while waiting for Radha. As Radha arrived, Krishna addressed Her with the utmost tenderness, saying, "O Radha, You are the queen of My heart and the essence of My existence. Without You, the pastimes of Vrundavan are incomplete."

To honor Radha, Krishna led Her to a sacred grove, Govind Kund, where they sat beneath a Kadamba tree. There, Krishna played His flute, and the melody became a conversation of love, symbolizing their divine union. The cows, sensing their harmony, grazed peacefully, and the entire forest seemed to rejoice in their blissful interaction.

In this leela, Radha lovingly calls Krishna Govind because He takes care of the cows with love.

He satisfies the spiritual needs of all devotees, including Herself.

His flute rules the hearts of all, including Radha Herself. Krishna, in return, accepts the name Radha Govind to reflect that His supreme joy lies in Radha's love and devotion.

The other leela that has a direct connection with Radha Govind happens during the prelude of Raas Lila. Krishna, playing his flute, summons the gopis to the Yamuna River. But this time, He only devotes most of His attention to Radha.

Krishna proclaims, "O Radha, You are My dearest one, the

cause of My being. Though I am Govind, the preserver and feeder of the world, You are the one that gives meaning to My divine play." Radha, in return, says Krishna is the real Govind as He takes proper care of the cows and the devotees.

Their association reflects Krishna's timelessness with Radha, and thus He is known as Radha Govind, the Lord of Radha.

Radha represents unconditional love and devotion, and Govind is Krishna's role as the divine protector and fulfiller of spiritual desires. Together, Radha Govind reflects the bond of love that cannot be separated between God and His devotee.

Krishna's love towards cows, natural elements, and His devotees reflects divine harmony. This name helps in respecting nature and fostering compassion for everyone.

It is through Krishna's grace and Radha's bhakti that the very purpose of human life-to united with the ultimate reality is satisfied.

5. Radhakanta (Beloved of Radha)

Leela- Maan Leela

Krishna, known as Radhakanta, the beloved of Radha, epitomizes the divine love that transcends the material world and reflects the highest spiritual union. The leelas involving Radha and Krishna are the most celebrated, highlighting the pure, unconditional, and eternal love between the divine couple.

As we know, Radha and Krishna's love is not just a romantic tale but a profound spiritual allegory representing the soul's deep yearning and ultimate union with the divine. Their love is portrayed through numerous enchanting leelas in Vrundavan, each illustrating the depth and intensity of their relationship.

Another leela that exemplifies Krishna as Radhakanta is the incident of Radha's anger, known as Maan Leela. Once, Radha felt neglected as Krishna's attention was towards other gopis. She withdrew Herself in a state of sulk or maan. Krishna, deeply devoted to Radha, sought to appease Her by performing various acts of humility and charm. He decorated Himself with flowers and peacock feathers, sang sweet songs, and even knelt before Her, begging for forgiveness. Radha's maan eventually melted in the face of Krishna's sincere devotion, and They reunited in joyous harmony.

These leelas underscore that Radha and Krishna's love transcends physical boundaries and is a manifestation of divine love, free from any material imperfections. Radha's devotion and surrender to Krishna exemplify the ideal relationship between the Soul and the Supreme Being. The intensity of Radha's love and Krishna's reciprocation highlight the mutual exchange of love between the Devotee and the Divine.

Through Their love, Radha and Krishna demonstrate the principles of selfless devotion, surrender, and the blissful union with the divine.

The leelas of Radhakanta teach that true love is selfless, pure, and eternal, beyond any material desires or limitations. Devotees seek to emulate Radha's intense devotion and Krishna's boundless love, aspiring to achieve a similar union with the divine in their spiritual journey. This divine love story continues to inspire countless devotees, providing a powerful symbol of the soul's ultimate goal: union with the beloved, the Supreme Divine.

The Madhurya Ras is highlighted in the graceful dance, the beauty of Krishna's movements, and the joyous laughter shared between Them.

6. Radha-Krishna (The Inseperable Divine)

Krishna is called Radha Krishna as Radha and Krishna are taken as the most prominent symbol of divine love and unity. Names are often said together to establish that they can never be separated. This establishes an eternal relationship between the individual soul (Radha) and Supreme Consciousness (Krishna). The name Radha Krishna conveys the idea that Krishna is not complete without Radha and vice versa; that is, the identity of Radha is the identity of Krishna.

The Divine Mirror Leela

Radha and Krishna were spending their day and night in the forests of Vrundavan. There were gopis everywhere and the beauty of nature. One day, while in this playful mood, Radha said, "You are the Supreme Lord. You save the whole universe. But you are always attached to me. What is the reason for that?"

Krishna smiled and took Radha to a crystal-clear lake nearby. They looked into the water, and Krishna pointed at their reflection, saying, "Look carefully, Radha. Can you see how I am incomplete without you? Wherever I go, you are always with me. My identity as Krishna exists only because of you. I am Radha Krishna, for we are eternally one."

To further explain His point, Krishna plucked a lotus flower and showed it to Radha. He said, "This flower's beauty lies in its petals and fragrance. The petals are you, and the fragrance is me. One cannot exist without the other. Similarly, we are two aspects of the same divine essence."

Radha smiled, realizing the depth of Krishna's words. The gopis who witnessed this divine exchange realized that Radha are not just two individuals but the perfect manifestation of the divine love and unity.

Leela-The Kundal Leela
One day when Radha was playing with her friends on the banks of the river Yamuna, Her earring fell into the river. She became distressed and worried about losing Her Kundal. On seeing Her concern, Krishan immediately promised to get them back for Her. Krishan dived into the river and pretended to search for the earrings. He lingered in the water to tease Radha by staying there longer than necessary.

Radha became anxious and started to call out for Krishna. Calling Krishna's name shows Her deep concern for Him Krishna emerged triumphantly holding the earring. He refused to return it. He mischievously asked Her to pay a price for retrieving it. He asked for her loving glance or a smile. Initially She hesitated but eventually smiled.

This leela signifies the playful and loving exchanges between Radha and Krishna. Radha's concern for Krishna shows extreme devotion of soul towards God. The Yamuna represents the flow of devotion and the kundal signifies the connection between the devotee (Radha) and the divine (Krishna).

Raas Leela

In the divine Raas leela, Krishna multiplied Himself to dance with each Gopi, yet Radha and Krishna danced together, symbolizing the inseparable bond between the divine lover and beloved. The Madhurya Ras, the sweet, loving flavor of their dance, radiated through the forest, making the moon shine brighter and the flowers bloom more vividly. This leela signifies the divine and romantic love that transcends the earthly realm, where Radha and Krishna's souls are intertwined in eternal bliss.

7. Radha Kunjabihari (The enjoyer of Groves)

Leela-The Mayur (peacock) Dance Leela

The name "Radha Kunjabihari" beautifully depicts the Mayur (peacock) Dance Leela of Radha and Krishna. The name "Kunjabihari" means "one who enjoys in the groves," highlighting Krishna's playful and joyful nature as He dances with Radha in these sacred groves.

This leela captures the essence of divine love and the natural beauty of Vrundavan, where Radha and Krishna's dance with the peacocks becomes a symbol of their eternal, blissful union. The Mayur Dance Leela is a reminder of the joyous and playful relationship between Radha and Krishna, celebrated by devotees through dance, music, and devotion.

The name "Radha Kunjabihari" is a profound representation of the enchanting and divine relationship between Radha and Krishna, particularly embodied in the Mayur (peacock) Dance Leela. This name encapsulates Krishna's playful and joyous nature, as He delights in the beauty of the Vrundavan groves, or kunjas, while in the divine company of Radha. The imagery associated with this name is deeply symbolic and evocative, conjuring visions of their ethereal dance that transcends the physical realm and enters the sphere of divine love and devotion.

In the sacred groves of Vrundavan, Radha and Krishna's love plays out like a celestial dance, where every movement is imbued with deep spiritual significance. The groves, or kunjas, themselves are symbolic of the sanctified spaces where the divine couple's love flourishes, untouched by the worries and concerns of the material world. These lush, green environments are alive with the fragrance of flowers, the song of birds, and the vibrant colors of peacocks, all contributing to the atmosphere of divine bliss that envelops Radha and Krishna. It is in this serene and sacred environment that the Mayur Dance Leela takes place, where Krishna, adorned with peacock feathers, engages in a dance that celebrates both the beauty of nature and the profound bond He shares with Radha.

The Mayur Dance Leela is not just a physical dance; it is a manifestation of the divine joy and love that Radha and Krishna share. As Krishna dances with Radha, the peacocks join in, spreading their vibrant feathers in a display of nature's beauty that mirrors the splendor of the divine couple's love. The sound of Krishna's flute fills the air, its melody weaving through the trees and flowers, creating a symphony that speaks directly to the hearts of those who witness it. Radha, in turn, moves gracefully beside Krishna, Her every step a testament to the perfect harmony that exists between them.

Krishna is not just a deity who resides in the lofty heavens; He is intimately connected to the natural world and finds joy in the simple, yet profound pleasures of life. His love for Radha is expressed not through grand gestures but through these moments of shared joy in the beauty of Vrundavan's groves. It is this connection to both the divine and the natural world that makes Krishna accessible to His devotees, who see in Him not just a god to be worshipped from afar, but a beloved friend and lover who revels in the same joys and sorrows that they do.

The Mayur Dance Leela is a celebration of this divine union, where the boundaries between the human and the divine blur, allowing Radha and Krishna to connect on the deepest of levels. Their dance is a metaphor for the eternal, blissful union that exists between the soul and the divine—a union that is not constrained by time or space but is ever-present and ever-joyful.

8.Radha Madhav (Embodiment of Divine Love)

Leela- Symbol of Divine Union

Radha is the foremost and beloved consort of Krishna, symbolizing the highest form of devotion and love.

Madhav is one of Krishna's many names, meaning "the one who is born in the family of Madhu" (a name of the Yadu dynasty) or "the Lord of the Madhu (honey-like) qualities."

Radhamadhav thus signifies "Krishna, the beloved of Radha" or "Krishna, who is the essence of sweetness and devotion."

The name "Radha Madhav" also captures the essence of this divine relationship. "Madhav" is another name for Krishna, emphasizing His role as the beloved of Radha. This name underscores the deep affection and eternal connection that binds them. Radha and Madhav are inseparable, two halves of the same divine essence. Where Radha represents the supreme devotee, the epitome of love and devotion, Madhav symbolizes the divine beloved who is both the object of devotion and the source of divine love.

The significance of these names and the leelas they represent is not limited to the past; they continue to resonate with devotees today. Through the names "Radha Kunjabihari" and "Radha

Madhav," devotees are reminded of the ideal of divine love—a love that is pure, selfless, and eternal. The stories and leelas associated with these names inspire devotees to cultivate these qualities in their own lives, to see the divine in the world around them, and to experience the joy of being in the presence of the divine, just as Radha and Krishna do in the groves of Vrundavan.

In essence, these names and leelas are living traditions that continue to inspire and uplift the hearts of those who seek a deeper connection with the divine. They remind us that divine love is not just something to be read about or remembered; it is something to be experienced and lived, in every moment, and in every breath.

The name Radha Madhav highlights the eternal and transcendental love between Krishna and Radha. It represents the ultimate expression of divine love and devotion, where Radha embodies the purest form of bhakti (devotion) and Krishna is the beloved deity.

Radha Madhav symbolizes the perfect union of the divine masculine (Madhav/Krishna) and feminine (Radha) principles. This union is seen as a reflection of the perfect harmony and balance in the universe.

Devotees who chant or meditate on the name Radha Madhav often seek to deepen their understanding and experience of divine love and devotion. It serves as a reminder of the intimate relationship between the devotee (Radha) and the divine (Madhav/Krishna).

9. Radha Madan Mohan (One Who enchants Madan-cupid)

Leela- Krishna enchants Madan, the Cupid

The name Radha Madan Mohan literally means "Radha's Krishna, who enchants even Cupid (Madan)". Krishna is called Madan Mohan because He enchants not only the minds of devotees but also Kamadeva-Cupid, the god of love. With Radha, this name emphasizes their divine love wherein Krishna becomes the embodiment of supreme attraction and Radha the epitome of devotion.

The name signifies that though Krishna enchants everyone, He Himself is enchanted by Radha's unconditional love and devotion.

One of the leelas associated with the name Radha Madan Mohan revolves around Krishna's divine ability to enchant and transcend worldly desires.

Krishna's beauty and charm are strong enough to capture not only humans and gods but even abstract things such as desire and attraction (Madan). Once, Kamadeva, the god of love, became proud of his power to enthrall everyone, even the gods. Hearing about Krishna's beauty that is beyond material attachment, Kamadeva decided to test Krishna's charm. He came to Vrundavan and released his most potent arrows of love to affect Krishna. But Krishna was not affected; he was engaged in His divine play with Radha and the gopis.

Thus, with Krishna's spellbound form and interaction with Radha, Kamadeva felt humiliated and overpowered. Kamadeva understood that Krishna, Madan Mohan, is more than averse to materialistic attraction but he himself is the very fountainhead of spiritual love beyond all wishes.

Radha, however, who had witnessed Krishna's superiority even over Kamadeva, called Him lovingly Madan Mohan, for Krishna enchants the enchanter but is captivated by Radha's pure love. This leela emphasizes that Krishna transcends material attraction and embodies divine, selfless love.

Radha Madan Mohan symbolizes the divine love between Radha and Krishna, where Krishna enchants all beings, yet remains captivated by Radha's devotion. This leela reminds devotees to seek spiritual love.

Krishna lovingly called Radha Madan Mohan Mohini, meaning "the enchantress of the enchanter of Cupid," as her unparalleled devotion and beauty captivated even Krishna, who enchants all creation.

10. Radha Ramana (The one who gives joy to Radha)

Leela-The Yamuna Play

Once, while playing on the banks of the Yamuna River, Krishna teased Radha by hiding Her favorite flower garland. Radha, in Her playful anger, refused to speak to Krishna. To win back her affection, Krishna playfully created various tricks and illusions, making Radha laugh. This leela signifies the playful and loving nature of Their relationship, where Krishna always seeks to bring joy to Radha. The Madhurya Ras here is shown in the light-hearted teasing and the deep affection Krishna has for Radha, always finding ways to make Her smile and feel cherished.

In the lush and tranquil surroundings of Vrundavan, Radha and Krishna's playful exchanges were the very heart of Their divine love. On another delightful day by the Yamuna River, Krishna decided to engage in a new game with Radha and the gopis. As they gathered to pick flowers and enjoy each other's company, Krishna, ever the playful enchanter, decided to test Radha's affection in a unique way.

Krishna, knowing that Radha adored the sight of peacocks, used His divine powers to create a stunning display. He summoned a group of peacocks, whose vibrant plumage spread out like a living, colorful carpet. The birds began to dance in a circle around Radha, their movements synchronized with the sweet melodies Krishna played on His flute. The sight was mesmerizing, and Radha's heart swelled with joy as She watched the peacocks twirl and sway to the rhythm of the flute.

However, Krishna had more in store. As the peacocks danced, He used His mystical abilities to vanish from Radha's sight, leaving Her surrounded by the dancing birds but without Her beloved Krishna in view. At first, Radha was puzzled, Her eyes searching for Krishna amidst the flurry of colors and movement. Her heart, always attuned to His presence, began to yearn for Him even more intensely.

Sensing Her growing anticipation, Krishna reappeared suddenly, this time dressed in a peacock-feathered outfit, blending in seamlessly with the peacocks around Him. His dark complexion, paired with the vibrant hues of the feathers, made Him look like the king of peacocks—a sight that left Radha spellbound. Krishna then danced alongside the peacocks, mimicking their movements with such grace and precision that it became difficult to tell Him apart from the birds.

This playful disguise delighted Radha, who recognized Her beloved in the midst of His divine mischief. She laughed heartily, Her earlier displeasure forgotten, as she watched Krishna move with the elegance and freedom of the peacocks. The dance turned into a celebration of their love, with Radha joining in, twirling and laughing in pure bliss.

After the dance, Krishna, still adorned with peacock feathers, approached Radha with a garland of freshly picked flowers. He placed it around Her neck as a gesture of His unending love and devotion. The gopis, who had been watching from a distance, joined in the joyous moment, clapping and singing praises of the divine couple.

This leela highlights Krishna's playful and loving nature, where He constantly finds creative ways to bring joy to Radha and express His deep affection for Her. The Madhurya Ras, or sweet rasa, is vividly displayed here, not just in the light-hearted teasing but in the profound connection that underlies all Their interactions. Krishna's ability to surprise and enchant Radha, to turn even the simplest of moments into a divine spectacle, reflects the depth of Their love—a love that is both playful and deeply spiritual.

In this leela, the peacock feathers also symbolize Krishna's role as the protector and nurturer of all creation, with His dance representing the cosmic play of the universe. Yet, even amidst this grand display, Krishna's focus remains solely on Radha, underscoring the intimate and personal nature of Their divine relationship. This enchanting episode, like many others, showcases the inseparable bond between Radha and Krishna, a bond that continues to inspire and captivate the hearts of devotees.

11. Radhika Pati (The consort of Radhika (Radha)

Leela- Bhandirvan- marriage of Radha-Krishna

Garga-Samhita tells of Radha and Krishna as children, walking together along the blue waters of the Yamuna in Vrundavan. They stopped to rest under the shade of a Banyan tree when, through the influence of Yogamaya, they suddenly took on their youthful forms. Lord Brahma appeared out of nowhere and, acting as the priest, performed a symbolic wedding ceremony for Radha and Krishna, with the demigods in attendance. During the ceremony, Radha's sari and Krishna's dhoti were tied together, as is customary in Vedic weddings. Afterwards, they returned to their childhood forms and walked home together. This leela, where the Divine Couple is symbolically bound together, is also celebrated by some Vaishnavas as the pastime of Radha-Damodara.

Leela-The Boat Ride

One tranquil day in Vrundavan, the divine couple, Radha and Krishna, decided to enjoy the serene beauty of the Yamuna River by taking a boat ride. The sun was gently descending, casting a golden hue across the water, and the river seemed to flow more softly in anticipation of the love-filled adventure that was about to unfold. The gentle ripples of the Yamuna glimmered like jewels, reflecting the beauty of the lush greenery and the colorful flowers that adorned its banks. The entire scene was set as if nature itself was preparing to witness another enchanting leela of Radha and Krishna.

As Radha and Krishna stepped into the beautifully decorated boat, it gently rocked on the calm waters. The boat was adorned with fragrant flowers, soft cushions, and intricate designs that made it a perfect setting for their divine journey. Krishna, with his mischievous smile, took the oars and began rowing, his eyes constantly stealing glances at Radha, who was seated gracefully, her delicate hands resting on her lap, adorned with bangles that jingled softly with the boat's movements.

The boat glided smoothly on the river, surrounded by the soothing sounds of nature—the gentle flow of water, the melodious chirping of birds, and the soft rustle of leaves in the breeze. Radha and Krishna were in complete harmony with Their surroundings, as if the very elements were celebrating Their presence. The calm and quietude of the Yamuna River provided the perfect backdrop for this intimate moment, allowing the couple to lose Themselves in each other's company.

As They sailed further into the river, Krishna's playful nature began to surface. He slowly started to rock the boat from side to side, creating gentle waves that made the boat sway. Radha, startled by the sudden movement, looked at Krishna with a mix of surprise and playful annoyance. Krishna, feigning innocence, continued to rock the boat, His laughter resonating through the air. Radha, trying to maintain Her balance, instinctively reached out and held onto Krishna for support.

The moment Radha clung to Krishna, a wave of warmth and affection swept over them both. The boat, now swaying more vigorously, became a symbol of their playful yet deeply affectionate relationship. Radha, with her heart pounding, half in fear and half in the thrill of the moment, couldn't help but laugh along with Krishna. Their laughter echoed across the Yamuna, blending with the natural symphony of the river and the forest, creating a melody of love and joy.

In that moment, the rocking boat wasn't just a playful prank by Krishna; it became a metaphor for the ebb and flow of their relationship, full of moments of excitement, slight fears, and overwhelming love. The Madhurya Ras, the essence of sweet love, was vividly expressed in the way they held onto each other—Radha's delicate hands gripping Krishna's arms tightly, and Krishna's strong yet gentle hold reassuring Her of His presence. The thrill of the swaying boat brought Them closer, both physically and emotionally, as They shared this intimate moment of vulnerability and trust.

As the boat ride continued, Krishna, sensing Radha's comfort and ease, gradually slowed down the rocking. The boat settled into a gentle glide once again, allowing Them to relax and enjoy the peaceful surroundings. Radha, now resting against Krishna, felt a sense of security and bliss. They sat close together, Their hearts beating in unison, as They took in the beauty of the river and the enchanting landscape that stretched out before them.

The surrounding nature seemed to celebrate Their love—flowers blooming more vibrantly, birds singing more sweetly, and even the Yamuna's waters appearing to flow with a softer, more loving caress. The boat ride, initially filled with playful mischief, transitioned into a serene journey where Radha and Krishna could simply be together, sharing the beauty of nature and the depths of their affection.

In the quiet moments that followed, Radha and Krishna exchanged tender glances, their eyes reflecting the love they held for each other. The boat, now gently drifting with the current, became a sanctuary of peace and love, where words were unnecessary, and their hearts spoke the language of pure devotion. The surrounding world faded away, leaving only the divine couple and the boundless love they shared.

As the boat ride came to an end and They approached the riverbank, Radha and Krishna stepped out, Their hands still intertwined. The leela on the Yamuna River wasn't just a simple boat ride; it was a profound expression of the Madhurya Ras that permeated their relationship. It highlighted the playful yet deeply loving bond They shared, where even the smallest moments became an opportunity to connect on a deeper level.

This leela reminds devotees that love is not just about grand gestures but also about the small, tender moments of joy, laughter, and shared experiences. The serene beauty of nature, combined with the playful dynamics of Radha and Krishna's relationship, made this boat ride a timeless symbol of divine love, celebrated in the hearts of all who hear this enchanting tale.

12. Radha Priya (One Who Loves Radha)

Leela- The Peacock Feather Garland

Radha Priya, meaning "the beloved of Radha," is a name that reflects Krishna's inseparable bond and intimate relationship with Radha. This name signifies Krishna's immense love for Radha, where she holds the highest position in His heart. The leela associated with this name beautifully illustrates how Krishna treasures Radha above all and expresses the divine interplay of love between them.

One day, Radha and Krishna, along with the gopis, were spending their time in the lush groves of Vrundavan .

The gopis started playfully teasing Krishna, asking Him if He loved Radha more than anyone else. "Krishna, you say Radha is special to You, but how can we know for sure? Do You love Her more than anyone else?"

With a mischievous smile on His face, He decided to show them how dear Radha was to Him. He took a few peacock feathers from the surroundings and started stringing them into an exquisite garland. As He was stringing it, He filled the garland with all His love and devotion and began muttering Radha's name in a whisper.

Once the garland was made, Krishna put it on Radha's head with great devotion and bowed to Her, declaring, "Radha is My dearest! I exist only to serve her joy. If I am Krishna, then She is My very soul. I am Radha Priya because Her love sustains Me."

The gopis, overwhelmed by Krishna's display of affection and humility, realized that Radha's devotion was unparalleled, and Krishna's love for Her was eternal and unique. This leela immortalized Krishna as Radha Priya, the one who treasures Radha above all.

In another leela, Radha once playfully demanded proof of Krishna's love. Krishna, delighted by Her teasing, said, "I will prove My love in the most unique way." He dived into the Yamuna River and collected the most fragrant lotus flowers, which He wove into a garland.

Returning to Radha, Krishna put the garland around Her neck and said, "You are My beloved, Radha Priya. Just as these lotus flowers cannot bloom without sunlight, My life has no meaning without Your love. You are My heart, My soul, and My eternal joy."

It is in these touching words that the joyful tears welled up in the eyes of Radha, and thus, the Vrundavan grove vibrated with divine love from Radha and Krishna.

Spiritual Implication of the Name Radha Priya
Radha, is the Personification of Bhakti. She symbolizes the purest form of devotion, as the love from Krishna manifests the fact that the Divine admires pure selfless devotion most of all.

Krishna's name Radha Priya teaches that God is not merely distant, nor unconcerned, but indeed deeply involved in a loving relationship with the soul, represented by Radha.

This name also symbolizes the bond of indivisibility of a devotee with the divine and hence teaches that true love and surrender bring unity with God.

Krishna's humility and devotion to Radha illustrate that divine love transcends ego and hierarchy, emphasizing mutual respect and joy.

Krishna is called Radha Priya because He is eternally devoted to Radha and treasures her above all. The leelas associated with this name highlight the depth of their divine love, which symbolizes the eternal connection between the soul and the

Divine. It reminds devotees that pure devotion is the ultimate path to experiencing God's love and grace.
Radha and Krishna are not just two individuals but the perfect manifestation of divine love and unity.

Another Leela: The Name of the Universe
In another leela, Radha once asked Krishna why her name was always mentioned with His. Krishna replied, "Radha, you are my very life. You are the one who makes me who I am. Without you, my name would not hold the same power."

This he demonstrated by engraving the word "Radha" on His chest with a kusha blade. He told her, "Your name will not be separate from mine from this day forward. When anyone calls upon me as Krishna, he will also be calling upon you as Radha Krishna, for we are one soul in two bodies.

The inseparability of Devotee and Divine: The name Radha Krishna represents the eternal unity between the devotee (Radha) and the Divine (Krishna).

Symbol of Pure Love: Their relationship symbolizes the highest form of love, which is unconditional, selfless, and spiritual.

Unity of Shakti and Shaktimaan: Radha represents Shakti

(divine energy), while Krishna is Shaktimaan (the wielder of energy). Together, they complete the cosmos.

Divine Mirror: The reflection in the water signifies that the soul, Radha, and the Supreme, Krishna, are two sides of the same coin and can never be separated.

13. Radha Shyam (Radha's dark-hued beloved)

Leela- Gopis teasing Krishna

One of the most beautiful leelas associated with this name is Krishna's love for Radha and the love They both share for each other.

Once, the gopis gathered in Vrundavan and playfully asked Krishna why Radha is so special to Him. They teased Him about how He, the Supreme Lord, always follows Radha and is completely devoted to Her. Krishna, smiling, decided to demonstrate the unique nature of Their bond.

Krishna took the gopis to the banks of the Yamuna, where He asked them to look at His reflection in the water. To their surprise, they saw Radha's name on Krishna's chest and Her picture reflected in His eyes all the time. Krishna said, "Radha lives in My heart, and Her love guides all My actions. She is My very life, and I am called Shyam because of Her devotion to Me. Without Radha, there is no Shyam."

At the divine play, gopis understood that Krishna and Radha are not separated from each other and, thus, are eternal unions of the soul (Radha) and the Divine (Krishna).

In another leela, Krishna, out of mischief, spent time playfully teasing the gopis, which made Radha upset. She went into maan, a loving sulk, and refused to speak to Krishna. Feeling incomplete without Her, Krishna approached Her with humility and devotion. To please Her, He adorned Himself with peacock feathers, garlands, and ornaments, calling Himself "Radha Shyam"—proclaiming that He exists only for Her.

His selfless act softened Radha's heart and Their love bloomed right there. Krishna's name became Radha Shyam, which did not only come to indicate Their connection but also revealed the significance of the leela.

There is a spiritual significance to this leela.

The name "Radha Shyam" symbolizes that Radha is not just a friend but the soul of Krishna; She represents pure devotion and love.

The leela teaches that the soul (Radha) and God (Krishna/Shyam) are eternally connected. The soul seeks the Divine, while the Divine is drawn to the soul's devotion.

Krishna, the Supreme Lord, humbles Himself before Radha, showing that love and devotion are the highest truths in the spiritual realm.

Through the name Radha Shyam, devotees remember and cherish the eternal, blissful love between Radha and Krishna, which goes beyond the world of matter and is an ideal of divine union.

14. Radhavallabh (The Divine Lover of Radha)

Leela-The Swing Festival

During the monsoon season, Radha and Krishna would participate in the swing festival. Krishna would push the swing on which Radha sat, and together They would enjoy the festive atmosphere with songs and laughter. The gentle movements of the swing, coupled with the rhythmic sound of the raindrops, created an ambiance of pure joy and love. This leela illustrates the intimate moments of joy and affection shared between Radha and Krishna, highlighting their deep emotional connection. The Madhurya Ras is evident in Their shared laughter, the tender glances, and the sweet conversations that passed between them.

The Swing Festival, also known as *Jhulan Yatra*, is a beautiful and cherished festival that takes place during the monsoon season, celebrating the divine love between Radha and Krishna. This festival, which typically occurs in the month of Shravan, brings to life one of the most tender and joyous pastimes of Radha and Krishna. The atmosphere during this time is infused with the scent of wet earth, the lush greenery of Vrundavan, and the rhythmic sound of raindrops, all of which create the perfect setting for this divine leela.

In this enchanting festival, Radha and Krishna participate in the swing rituals, symbolizing the playful and loving relationship they share. The swing, adorned with flowers, garlands, and vibrant fabrics, becomes the focal point of the celebration. Radha, dressed in Her finest attire, takes Her seat on the swing, Her eyes sparkling with anticipation. Krishna, ever the playful lover, stands beside Her, His heart brimming with affection and joy.

As the swing begins to move, gently pushed by Krishna, the world seems to pause in awe of the divine couple. The movements of the swing are synchronized with the rhythm of the raindrops, creating a melody that resonates with the hearts of all who witness it. The gentle back-and-forth motion of the swing symbolizes the ebb and flow of emotions between Radha and Krishna, each push a testament to the love that binds them together.

The Swing Festival is not merely a physical event; it is a spiritual celebration of love, joy, and togetherness. As Krishna pushes the swing, Radha's laughter fills the air, a sound so pure and joyful that it seems to make the flowers bloom more vibrantly, the rain fall more sweetly, and the birds sing more melodiously. Krishna, captivated by Radha's beauty and happiness, cannot take His eyes off Her. Their tender glances, exchanged amidst the swinging motion, speak volumes of the deep emotional connection they share. It is in these moments that the

Madhurya Ras, the sweet and intimate mood of divine love, is most palpable.

During the festival, the residents of Vrundavan, the Gopis and Gopas, gather around to witness this divine spectacle. They sing devotional songs, known as *Jhulan* songs, which recount the playful and loving pastimes of Radha and Krishna. The lyrics of these songs, filled with adoration and reverence, add to the festive atmosphere, making the celebration even more joyous. The Gopis, who share an unparalleled love and devotion for Radha and Krishna, join in the festivities, taking turns to push the swing, eager to be a part of this sacred moment.

The swing itself becomes a symbol of the balance and harmony that Radha and Krishna bring to each other's lives. Just as the swing moves gracefully between two points, their love too swings between moments of playful teasing and deep affection. This balance is what makes their relationship so unique and divine. Krishna, with his mischievous nature, often teases Radha during the swing festival, whispering sweet nothings into her ear, or pretending to push the swing too fast, only to catch her in his arms. Radha, though sometimes feigning annoyance, is secretly delighted by Krishna's antics, Her heart swelling with love for Him.

As the festival continues, the swing becomes not just a physical object but a metaphor for the ups and downs of life, where love acts as the stabilizing force. Radha and Krishna, through their participation in the Swing Festival, demonstrate that true love is about enjoying each other's company, finding joy in the simplest of moments, and creating memories that transcend time.

In the end, the Swing Festival is more than just a celebration of a season; it is a celebration of love in its purest form. It reminds devotees that the divine love between Radha and Krishna is not just an ideal to be admired but an experience to be cherished and emulated in their own lives. Through the gentle swings, the shared laughter, and the tender glances, Radha and Krishna invite Their devotees into Their world of eternal bliss, where every moment is filled with the sweetness of love and the joy of togetherness.

15. Radhavihari (The one who enchants Radha)

Leela-The Forest Picnic

In the serene and verdant forests of Vrundavan, Radha and Krishna, along with Their close friends, often indulged in delightful picnics that embodied the purest joy and love. The picnics were not just ordinary gatherings but divine celebrations of Their eternal bond, filled with laughter, music, and playful moments that brought immense joy to everyone present.

As the group walked through the lush greenery of Vrundavan, the beauty of nature surrounded Them. The fragrance of blooming flowers, the melodious chirping of birds, and the gentle rustling of leaves created a perfect setting for their divine rendezvous. The Yamuna River flowed gracefully nearby, adding to the tranquility of the scene, while the cool breeze whispered through the trees, enhancing the enchanting atmosphere.

Krishna, with His enchanting flute, would often lead the way, playing melodious tunes that captivated everyone's hearts. Radha, deeply absorbed in Krishna's presence, walked beside Him, Her heart overflowing with love and admiration. Their friends, the gopis and gopas, followed Them, singing and clapping their hands in rhythm to Krishna's flute, their spirits lifted by the divine music.

Upon reaching a beautiful clearing in the forest, shaded by ancient trees, they would settle down to enjoy the day together. The gopis, with their loving hands, would spread out soft blankets on the grass, while others arranged an assortment of delicious foods they had brought along. The picnic was a time of sharing, not just food, but also their innermost feelings, stories, and laughter.

Krishna, always eager to see Radha smile, would engage in playful antics, teasing Her and making Her laugh. He would sometimes take a morsel of food and offer it to Radha with a mischievous grin, or secretly swap Her plate with His, making everyone burst into laughter. Radha, although initially pretending to be annoyed by Krishna's pranks, could never resist His charm and would eventually join in the laughter, Her heart lightened by His love.

The group would then break into songs, singing praises of Krishna's divine qualities and the beauty of their surroundings. Radha's melodious voice, filled with love and devotion, would blend harmoniously with Krishna's flute, creating music that resonated with the very soul of nature. The trees, flowers, and even the river seemed to respond to their music, swaying and flowing in rhythm, as if acknowledging the divine love being expressed.

After the singing, Krishna would often suggest a dance, leading Radha and Their friends in a joyous celebration of life and love. The gopis would dance gracefully, their anklets jingling in perfect harmony with Krishna's flute. Radha, the embodiment of divine beauty, would dance with Krishna, Their movements perfectly synchronized, reflecting Their deep emotional connection. The dance would often culminate in a moment of stillness, where Radha and Krishna would gaze into each other's eyes, the world around them fading away as They lost themselves in Their love.

As the day progressed, They would all sit together, sharing stories and anecdotes from Their lives. Krishna, with His witty humor, would narrate tales that left everyone in splits, while Radha would share Her thoughts and feelings, always deep and full of wisdom. The exchange of stories would strengthen Their bond, creating memories that would be cherished for eternity.

The Madhurya Ras, or the sweet, intimate aspect of divine love, was beautifully woven into every moment of these picnics. Whether it was in the joyous singing, the playful dancing, or the deep contentment that Radha felt in Krishna's presence, the essence of Their divine love was always evident. These picnics were more than just gatherings; they were sacred moments where the divine love of Radha and Krishna blossomed, touching the hearts of all who were present and leaving an indelible mark on the very soul of Vrundavan.

These playful and joyous gatherings, rich in the sweetness of divine love, continue to inspire devotees to this day, reminding them of the pure, blissful love that exists between Radha and Krishna, a love that transcends time and space.

The leelas of Radha and Krishna are timeless tales of divine love, devotion, and joy. Each name of Krishna associated with Radha highlights a unique aspect of their relationship, demonstrating the depth and beauty of their eternal bond. These stories inspire devotees to seek a deeper connection with the divine through love, devotion, and surrender.

Chapter 3: Importance of Chanting Krishna's Names

In the Vedic tradition, the practice of chanting the names of Krishna, known as Nama Sankirtana or Japa, is considered one of the most potent forms of devotion. This practice is not merely a ritualistic repetition but a profound spiritual exercise that offers multifaceted benefits, ranging from personal spiritual upliftment to the deepening of one's connection with the Divine, and the cleansing of the heart and mind. Let us explore these benefits in detail.

Spiritual Upliftment: How Chanting Krishna's Names Elevate the Soul

Transcending Material Boundaries:

Chanting Krishna's name helps devotees rise above the mundane, materialistic concerns of daily life. The sacred vibrations of the names of the Lord are believed to have a transcendental nature that can transport the chanter to a higher plane of consciousness. In this elevated state, the soul can experience its true, eternal nature, beyond the physical and mental limitations imposed by the material world.

Path to Liberation:

The ultimate goal of spiritual practice in the Vedic tradition is moksha, or liberation from the cycle of birth and death. The Bhagavad Gita, one of the foundational texts of Hindu philosophy, states that chanting the holy names of God is a direct means to attain liberation. By constantly remembering and reciting Krishna's names, the soul becomes detached from material entanglements and drawn toward spiritual enlightenment.

Awakening Dormant Divinity:

Each soul is inherently divine, but this divinity is often covered by ignorance and material desires. Chanting Krishna's names awakens the dormant spiritual consciousness within. As a result, the devotee begins to see the world from a higher perspective, recognizing the presence of the Divine in all aspects of life.

Divine Grace and Protection:

The act of chanting Krishna's names is seen as a call to the Divine, inviting Krishna's grace and protection. The Vishnu Sahasranama, a hymn praising a thousand names of Vishnu (Krishna), suggests that the mere recitation of these names brings divine blessings. This grace can manifest in various forms, such as inner peace, spiritual strength, and protection from negative influences.

Connection to the Divine: Enhancing One's Personal Relationship with Krishna

Building a Personal Relationship:

Chanting Krishna's names fosters a personal and intimate relationship with the Divine. Each name encapsulates a different aspect of Krishna's personality and pastimes, allowing devotees to connect with him on multiple levels. Whether meditating on Krishna's role as a loving child, a heroic warrior, or a compassionate friend, devotees can build a multifaceted relationship with him.

Expressions of Love and Devotion:

In the Bhakti tradition, chanting is an expression of love and devotion. The repetitive utterance of Krishna's name is akin to calling out to a beloved. This loving invocation is a way of expressing the devotee's heartfelt feelings and desires to be in the presence of the Lord. Over time, this practice deepens the emotional bond between the devotee and Krishna.

Divine Communication:

Chanting serves as a form of communication with the Divine. Just as prayers and rituals are ways to converse with God, chanting Krishna's name is a dialogue filled with spiritual longing and devotion. This communication helps in receiving divine guidance and inspiration, aiding the devotee in their spiritual journey.

Experiencing Divine Presence:

Through the sincere and consistent practice of chanting, devotees often report experiencing a tangible sense of Krishna's presence in their lives. This presence can be felt as a profound inner peace, joy, or even as direct divine intervention. Such experiences reinforce the devotee's faith and commitment to their spiritual path.

Cleansing the Heart: Removing Negative Qualities and Purifying the Mind

Eradicating Negative Emotions:

The human heart is often burdened with negative emotions such as anger, jealousy, greed, and fear. These emotions cloud the mind and hinder spiritual progress. Chanting Krishna's name is a powerful method for cleansing these impurities. The holy vibrations of Krishna's name act like a spiritual solvent, dissolving negativity and replacing it with positive, divine qualities.

Developing Virtuous Qualities:

As the negative qualities are cleansed, positive traits such as compassion, humility, patience, and love begin to flourish. The Srimad Bhagavatam states that the regular chanting of the holy names purifies the heart and leads to the development of divine qualities. This transformation is not only beneficial for spiritual growth but also enhances one's interactions and relationships in the material world.

Mental Clarity and Focus:

The practice of chanting requires concentration and mindfulness, which helps in improving mental clarity and focus. By repeatedly focusing on the sacred names, the mind becomes disciplined and less prone to distractions. This heightened focus can spill over into other areas of life, improving overall efficiency and effectiveness.

Emotional Healing:

Many devotees find that chanting Krishna's name brings emotional healing. The process of vocalizing sacred names with devotion and intention can release stored emotional pain and bring a sense of relief and comfort. This healing effect is akin to the soothing presence of a dear friend who listens and provides solace.

Purification of Intentions:

In the journey of life, one's intentions and desires often get tainted by selfish motives. Chanting Krishna's name purifies these intentions, aligning them with higher, selfless goals. As a result, the devotee's actions become more dharmic (righteous) and are performed with a sense of duty and service, rather than personal gain.

The practice of chanting Krishna's name is a profound spiritual exercise with multifaceted benefits. It serves as a means of spiritual upliftment, enabling devotees to transcend material limitations and connect with their true, divine nature. By fostering a personal and intimate relationship with Krishna, chanting deepens the devotee's devotion and love for the Divine, enhancing their spiritual experience.

Moreover, chanting acts as a powerful tool for cleansing the heart and mind. It eradicates negative qualities, cultivates positive virtues, and brings about emotional healing and mental clarity. This purification process not only aids in spiritual growth but also improves one's overall well-being and interactions in the material world.

In the Vedic tradition, names are sacred, and the names of Krishna encapsulate his divine qualities and pastimes. Chanting these names is not merely a ritualistic practice but a profound act of devotion and spiritual discipline. It is a pathway to divine grace, protection, and ultimate liberation. Through the sincere and regular practice of chanting Krishna's names, devotees can experience the transformative power of divine love, leading them closer to the ultimate goal of self-realization and union with the Divine.

Chapter 4: Bhavas

In the Vedic tradition, the act of naming is deeply sacred, and Krishna's numerous names reflect the infinite aspects of his divinity. Chanting these names is a powerful spiritual practice that not only brings the devotee closer to Krishna but also transforms the chanter, leading them towards the ultimate goal of self-realization and union with the divine.

In the devotional path of Bhakti Yoga, devotees relate to Krishna through various emotional states, known as "bhavas." These bhavas represent different kinds of relationships and attitudes towards the divine, allowing devotees to connect with Krishna in personal and intimate ways. The primary bhavas in which devotees view Krishna are:

- Shanta Bhava (Peaceful Love): In this mood, devotees appreciate Krishna's divine presence with a sense of reverence and tranquillity. There is a focus on Krishna's omnipresence and the peace that comes from acknowledging his divinity.

- Dasya Bhava (Servitude): Here, devotees see themselves as servants of Krishna. They derive joy and fulfillment from serving him, just as Hanuman served Lord Rama. This bhava emphasizes humility, duty, and devotion.

- Sakhya Bhava (Friendship): In this relationship, devotees see Krishna as their friend and companion. This bhava is characterized by familiarity, camaraderie, and equality, exemplified by Krishna's friendships with Arjuna and the cowherd boys of Vrundavan.

- Vatsalya Bhava (Parental Love): Devotees adopt the mood of a parent towards Krishna, expressing care, protection, and nurturing affection. This is the bhava of Yashoda and Nanda Maharaj, who loved Krishna as their own child.

- Madhurya Bhava (Conjugal Love): This is the most intimate and intense form of devotion, where devotees see Krishna as their beloved. It includes romantic and passionate love, as experienced by Radha and the gopis of Vrundavan. Madhurya Bhava is characterized by deep longing and loving exchanges with Krishna.

Each bhava offers a unique and personal way for devotees to experience and relate to Krishna, enriching their spiritual journey and deepening their connection with the divine.

Shanta Bhava: Prahlada

Story of Prahlada:

Prahlada, the son of the demon king Hiranyakashipu, is a renowned devotee of Lord Vishnu (Krishna). Despite being born into a family of asuras (demons), Prahlada possessed unwavering devotion to Vishnu from a very young age. His story is a prime example of Shanta Bhava, where his devotion was marked by a sense of peace, reverence, and transcendental calmness.

Hiranyakashipu, who considered himself the supreme ruler and despised Vishnu, was enraged by his son's devotion. He attempted numerous ways to dissuade Prahlada from worshipping Vishnu, but the young boy's faith remained unshaken. Hiranyakashipu subjected Prahlada to severe punishments, hoping to instil fear and obedience.

One of the most well-known attempts was when Hiranyakashipu tried to burn Prahlada alive by placing him on his sister Holika's lap, who had a boon making her immune to fire. However, due to Prahlada's steadfast faith, he emerged unscathed, while Holika was consumed by the flames.

Undeterred, Hiranyakashipu continued his efforts to kill Prahlada. He ordered his son to be thrown into a pit of snakes, trampled by elephants, poisoned, and even thrown off a cliff. Yet, each time, Prahlada was miraculously saved by Vishnu's grace.

Frustrated and furious, Hiranyakashipu confronted Prahlada and demanded to know where he derived his power. Prahlada calmly replied that Vishnu resided everywhere, in everything. Enraged, Hiranyakashipu asked if Vishnu was present in a nearby pillar. When Prahlada affirmed this, Hiranyakashipu struck the pillar, and out emerged Narasimha, the half-man, half-lion avatar of Vishnu.

Narasimha swiftly killed Hiranyakashipu, thus ending his tyrannical reign. Throughout these events, Prahlada remained serene and peaceful, embodying Shanta Bhava. His unwavering faith and tranquility in the face of adversity are celebrated as a testament to the power of devotion.

Impact on Devotees:

Prahlada's story teaches devotees the importance of unwavering faith and the peaceful surrender to divine will. It demonstrates that true devotion transcends fear and adversity. Devotees draw inspiration from Prahlada's calmness and his deep trust in Krishna's protection, learning to maintain their peace and devotion even in challenging circumstances.

Dasya Bhava: Hanuman

Story of Hanuman:

Though Hanuman is primarily known as a devotee of Lord Rama, he is also revered for his service to Krishna, an incarnation of Vishnu. Hanuman's devotion is characterized by Dasya Bhava, the mood of servitude, where he finds the ultimate joy in serving the Lord.

In one famous story, Hanuman's devotion to Krishna is highlighted when he meets Bhima during the Mahabharata. Bhima, another strong devotee of Krishna and one of the Pandavas encounters an old monkey while searching for a rare flower. The monkey, lying across the path, asks Bhima to move his tail if he wants to pass.

Bhima, confident in his strength, attempts to move the tail but is unable to budge it. Realizing that the monkey is no ordinary being, he humbly requests the monkey to reveal his true identity. The monkey then transforms into Hanuman and blesses Bhima, acknowledging their shared devotion to Krishna.

In another instance, during the Dwapara Yuga, Hanuman is said to have come to Vrundavan, where he encountered Krishna. Krishna, aware of Hanuman's deep devotion to Rama, took on the form of Rama to meet him. Overwhelmed with joy, Hanuman expressed his eternal service to the Lord, regardless of his incarnation.

Impact on Devotees:

Hanuman's unwavering dedication to serving Krishna exemplifies Dasya Bhava. His life teaches devotees the virtues of humility, loyalty, and selfless service. Devotees inspired by Hanuman strive to serve Krishna with the same dedication, seeing service as the highest form of devotion.

Sakhya Bhava: Arjuna

Story of Arjuna:

Arjuna, one of the Pandava princes and a central figure in the Mahabharata, is a prime example of Sakhya Bhava, where the devotee sees Krishna as a friend and companion. The bond between Arjuna and Krishna is characterized by deep friendship, trust, and mutual respect.

One of the most significant moments in Arjuna's life is the dialogue of the Bhagavad Gita. On the battlefield of Kurukshetra, Arjuna is filled with doubt and moral confusion about fighting in the war. Seeing his friend's turmoil, Krishna serves as his charioteer and guide.

Krishna imparts profound spiritual wisdom to Arjuna, addressing his concerns and guiding him towards his duty (dharma). Throughout the discourse, their relationship remains one of deep friendship. Krishna's role is not just as a divine teacher but also as a supportive friend, helping Arjuna navigate his inner conflicts.

In another instance, Krishna and Arjuna's friendship is evident during their adventures, such as retrieving a celestial weapon from the Khandava forest and the playful yet profound interactions they share. Krishna's involvement in Arjuna's life goes beyond just divine intervention; it showcases a relationship built on camaraderie and mutual support.

Impact on Devotees:

Arjuna's relationship with Krishna highlights the beauty of friendship with the divine. Devotees inspired by Sakhya Bhava seek to cultivate a personal, friendly relationship with Krishna, filled with trust and open-hearted communication. They learn to rely on Krishna not just as a deity but as a close friend who guides and supports them through life's challenges.

Vatsalya Bhava: Yashoda

Story of Yashoda:

Yashoda, the foster mother of Krishna, exemplifies Vatsalya Bhava, the mood of parental love. Her devotion is marked by deep affection, care, and nurturing love for Krishna, whom she raises as her own son.

One of the most beloved stories illustrating Vatsalya Bhava is the episode of Yashoda seeing the universe in Krishna's mouth. One day, while playing with his friends, young Krishna eats dirt. When Yashoda scolds Him and asks Him to open His mouth, she is astonished to see the entire cosmos within it. This divine vision reveals Krishna's supreme nature, yet Yashoda's motherly love remains unchanged. She continues to see Him as her little boy, demonstrating the depth of her parental affection.

Another popular story is when Yashoda tries to tie Krishna to a grinding mortar as punishment for His mischievous activities. Despite using all the ropes available, she finds them always a bit too short. This incident, known as Damodara

Leela, showcases her persistence and unconditional love, ultimately leading Krishna to allow himself to be bound by her love.

Impact on Devotees:

Yashoda's love for Krishna teaches devotees the importance of selfless, nurturing love. Her stories inspire parents to see their children as manifestations of the divine, fostering unconditional love and care. Devotees also learn that pure love transcends the recognition of divinity, focusing on the loving relationship itself.

Madhurya Bhava: Radha

Story of Radha:

Radha's love for Krishna epitomizes Madhurya Bhava, the mood of conjugal love. Her devotion is characterized by deep, passionate, and intimate love, making her the supreme devotee and beloved of Krishna.

Radha and Krishna's love is celebrated in countless stories, songs, and poems. One of the most enchanting tales is their nightly dance, the Rasa Leela, in the forests of Vrundavan.

During these dances, Krishna multiplies himself to dance with each gopi, yet his most intimate moments are shared with Radha. Their love transcends physical presence, symbolizing the soul's eternal bond with the divine.

In another story, Krishna leaves Vrundavan for Mathura, causing immense pain to Radha. Despite the physical separation, Radha's love for Krishna remains undiminished, highlighting the spiritual nature of their bond. Her devotion becomes a symbol of the soul's yearning and ultimate reunion with the divine.

Impact on Devotees:

Radha's devotion teaches devotees about the intensity and purity of divine love. Her unwavering love for Krishna, despite all obstacles, inspires devotees to cultivate a deep, personal, and intimate relationship with the divine. Radha's stories encourage a love that transcends material conditions, focusing on the eternal connection with Krishna.

Each bhava represents a unique way of relating to Krishna, enriching the devotional landscape. From the peaceful reverence of Prahlada, the servitude of Hanuman, the friendship of Arjuna, the parental love of Yashoda, to the passionate devotion of Radha, these stories highlight the diverse and profound relationships devotees can have with Krishna. They inspire devotees to find their personal path of devotion, deepening their spiritual connection and enriching their lives.

Chapter 5: Suggested Reading Materials on Krishna and His Names

For those interested in exploring the divine significance of Krishna and his numerous names, there are several revered books and scriptures that offer profound insights and spiritual wisdom. These texts not only illuminate Krishna's pastimes but also delve into the deeper meanings of his names and their impact on devotees. Here are some essential reading materials:

Bhagavad Gita

The Bhagavad Gita is a 700-verse Hindu scripture that is part of the Indian epic Mahabharata. It is a conversation between Prince Arjuna and the god Krishna, who serves as his charioteer. This sacred text addresses the moral and philosophical dilemmas faced by Arjuna on the battlefield of Kurukshetra. Krishna imparts spiritual wisdom and guidance, revealing his divine nature and various forms. The Gita emphasizes the importance of devotion (bhakti), righteous action (karma), and knowledge (jnana), making it a foundational text for understanding Krishna's multifaceted persona.

Srimad Bhagavatam (Bhagavata Purana)

The Srimad Bhagavatam is one of the most important Puranic texts in Hinduism. It consists of twelve cantos and over 18,000 verses, primarily focusing on the life and exploits of Lord Krishna. This scripture is considered the "ripened fruit" of the Vedic literature, offering detailed accounts of Krishna's childhood, youth, and various divine pastimes (leelas). Each story and name of Krishna mentioned in the Bhagavatam is imbued with deep spiritual significance, illustrating his qualities and attributes.

Garga Samhita

Garga Samhita is a revered ancient scripture attributed to Sage Garga. It is a comprehensive text that details the life and divine pastimes (leelas) of Lord Krishna. The text is divided into several sections, each focusing on different aspects of Krishna's life, including his childhood in Vrundavan, his interactions with the gopis, and his heroic deeds in Mathura and Dwarka. Garga Samhita also elaborates on the significance of Krishna's various names and forms, highlighting their spiritual meanings and benefits. This scripture is particularly valuable for devotees seeking a deeper understanding of Krishna's divine nature and the rich tapestry of his earthly activities.

Brahma Vaivarta Purana

Brahma Vaivarta Purana is one of the eighteen major Puranas in Hinduism. This extensive text is divided into four parts: Brahma Khanda, Prakriti Khanda, Ganesha Khanda, and Krishna Janma Khanda. The Krishna Janma Khanda is particularly significant as it focuses on the birth and exploits of Lord Krishna, detailing his pastimes in Vrundavan and his interactions with his devotees. The Purana emphasizes the concept of bhakti (devotion) and the power of Krishna's divine names and forms. It also discusses the creation of the universe and various mythological narratives, providing a holistic view of Hindu cosmology and theology. This scripture is cherished for its rich storytelling and deep spiritual insights, making it a vital text for Krishna devotees

Hari-Nama Cintamani

Hari-Nama Cintamani is a revered text written by Bhaktivinoda Thakur, a prominent Gaudiya Vaishnava theologian. This book is dedicated to the glories of the holy names of Krishna. It explains the process of chanting the Hare Krishna Maha Mantra and the transformative power it has on the practitioner's consciousness. The text delves into the significance of the different names of Krishna, the offences to avoid while chanting, and the stages of spiritual progress achieved through sincere chanting.

Sri Krishna Karnamrita

Sri Krishna Karnamrita is a beautiful work composed by Bilvamangala Thakura, a great saint and poet. This text is a collection of verses that vividly describe the enchanting beauty and divine pastimes of Lord Krishna. The poems are filled with deep devotion and love, capturing the essence of Krishna's charming nature and his playful interactions with the gopis (cowherd girls) of Vrundavan. The work emphasizes the sweetness (madhurya) of Krishna, making it a favorite among devotees who cherish his personal and intimate aspects.

Chaitanya Charitamrita

The Chaitanya Charitamrita, written by Krishnadasa Kaviraja Goswami, is a comprehensive biography of Lord Chaitanya Mahaprabhu, who is considered an incarnation of Krishna in the Gaudiya Vaishnavism tradition. This text not only recounts the life and teachings of Chaitanya Mahaprabhu but also highlights the importance of chanting Krishna's name as the most effective means of attaining spiritual enlightenment in the current age (Kali Yuga). It provides detailed explanations of the philosophy of Gaudiya Vaishnavism and the ecstatic experiences of devotees engaged in the congregational chanting of Krishna's names.

Nectar of Devotion (Bhakti-rasamrita-sindhu)

Written by Rupa Goswami, the Nectar of Devotion is a seminal text in the Bhakti movement. It systematically explains the science of devotion to Krishna, outlining the various stages and practices of bhakti. The text elaborates on the different names of Krishna, their meanings, and the specific moods (bhavas) with which devotees can approach him. It serves as a practical guide for devotees seeking to deepen their relationship with Krishna through loving devotion.

Sri Krishna Sandarbha

Authored by Jiva Goswami, one of the six Goswamis of Vrundavan, Sri Krishna Sandarbha is a part of the Sat Sandarbhas, a comprehensive philosophical treatise on the theology of Gaudiya Vaishnavism. This work specifically focuses on establishing Krishna as the Supreme Personality of Godhead. It provides a detailed analysis of Krishna's various names, forms, and pastimes, emphasizing his supremacy and the unique nature of his divine activities.

10. Bhagavata Mahatmya
Bhagavata Mahatmya is a section of the Padma Purana that extols the glories of the Srimad Bhagavatam and the chanting of Krishna's names. It contains stories and teachings that highlight the transformative power of engaging with Krishna's pastimes and reciting his names. The text assures devotees of the immense spiritual benefits and liberation that come from dedicatedly hearing and chanting about Krishna.

Govinda Leelamrita

Composed by Krishnadasa Kaviraja, Govinda Leelamrita describes the daily pastimes (asta kaliya leela) of Radha and Krishna in Vrundavan. This text immerses the reader in the intimate and loving exchanges between Krishna and his beloved gopis, particularly Radha. The work highlights the sweetness and joy of Krishna's names as they are invoked in the context of these divine pastimes.

Kṛṣṇa, The Supreme Personality of Godhead

It is a comprehensive book by A.C. Bhaktivedanta Swami Prabhupada, the founder of the International Society for Krishna Consciousness (ISKCON). This book, often referred to as the "Kṛṣṇa Book," is a detailed summary of the Tenth Canto of the Śrīmad Bhāgavatam. It vividly narrates the divine pastimes of Lord Krishna from his birth to his heroic feats and his interactions with his devotees. Prabhupada's work aims to make these spiritual stories accessible to a global audience, emphasizing Krishna's role as the Supreme Being and the essence of bhakti-yoga (devotional service).

These books and scriptures provide profound insights into the divine nature of Krishna and the significance of his names. They offer guidance on how to chant and meditate upon Krishna's names, revealing the transformative power of this devotional practice. By engaging with these texts, devotees can deepen their understanding of Krishna's divine pastimes, his multifaceted personality, and the immense spiritual benefits of chanting his holy names.

Importance of Devotional Songs and Bhajans

Devotional songs and bhajans hold a special place in the hearts of Krishna devotees. They are not just musical compositions but profound expressions of love, devotion, and surrender to the divine. Singing or listening to bhajans can transport the devotee into a state of spiritual ecstasy, providing a direct connection to Krishna.

Impacts of Bhajans

- Spiritual Upliftment: Bhajans elevate the soul, bringing the singer and listener closer to Krishna. The repetitive chanting and melodious tunes create a sacred atmosphere that fosters deep meditation and devotion.
- Cleansing the Heart: Singing bhajans helps purify the mind and heart. The divine names and stories of Krishna embedded in these songs remove negative thoughts and emotions, replacing them with positive and uplifting feelings.
- Community and Unity: Bhajans are often sung in groups, fostering a sense of community and unity among devotees. This collective singing experience strengthens bonds and shared devotion, creating a harmonious environment.
- Emotional Expression: Bhajans allow devotees to express their emotions freely. Whether it is joy, sorrow, love, or longing, these songs provide an outlet for expressing deep-seated feelings towards Krishna.
- Cultural Preservation: Bhajans play a crucial role in preserving and transmitting the rich cultural and

spiritual heritage associated with Krishna. They keep alive the traditions and teachings of great saints and poets.

Famous Bhajans and Their Emotions

1. "Achyutam Keshavam Krishna Damodaram"

अच्युतम केशवम कृष्ण दामोदरम्

राम नारायणम् जानकीवल्लभम्

This bhajan celebrates various names and forms of Lord Krishna, invoking a sense of reverence and adoration. It reflects the multifaceted nature of Krishna, acknowledging his roles as protector, lover, and divine incarnate. The repetition of these divine names induces a meditative state, filling the heart with devotion and peace.

2. "Shri Krishna Govind Hare Murari"

श्री कृष्ण गोविन्द हरे मुरारी

हे नाथ नारायण वासुदेवा

This bhajan calls out to Krishna, using his various epithets that highlight his divine qualities and pastimes. The chant-like nature of the song evokes a deep sense of surrender and longing. Devotees feel connected to Krishna's divine presence, experiencing his protection and grace.

3. "Hare Krishna Hare Krishna, Krishna Krishna Hare Hare"

हरे कृष्ण हरे कृष्ण, कृष्ण कृष्ण हरे हरे

हरे राम हरे राम, राम राम हरे हरे

This Maha Mantra is a powerful invocation of Krishna and Rama. It is a core practice in the Hare Krishna movement and is known for its ability to uplift the soul and purify the heart. Chanting this mantra brings peace, reduces stress, and fosters a direct connection with the divine.

4. "Maiya Mori Main Nahi Makhan Khayo"

मैया मोरी मैं नहीं माखन खायो

ब्रज में ढिंढोरा पियो पकड्यो न कन्हैया

This playful bhajan narrates the childhood leela of Krishna, where he denies stealing butter. It captures Krishna's mischievous and endearing personality, evoking joy and affection among devotees. Singing this bhajan brings a sense of playful intimacy with Krishna, reminiscent of his time in Vrundavan.

5. "Govind Bolo Hari Gopal Bolo"

गोविन्द बोलो हरी गोपाल बोलो

राधा रामण हारी गोविन्द बोलो

This bhajan is a simple yet profound invocation of Krishna's various names. The repetitive chanting instills a sense of calm and devotion. It encourages devotees to remember Krishna constantly, fostering a continuous meditative state and reinforcing the connection with the divine.

6. Adharam Madhuram

अधरं मधुरं वदनं मधुरं

नयनं मधुरं हसितं मधुरम्।

हृदयं मधुरं गमनं मधुरं

मधुराधिपतेरखिलं मधुरम्।।

"Adharam Madhuram" means "sweet are His lips". This bhajan glorifies the divine sweetness of Krishna, not just in his appearance but in his actions, words, and overall demeanor. It captures the essence of Krishna's divine charm and beauty, which enchants the hearts of his devotees. The repetition of "Madhuram" (sweet) reflects the indescribable and all-encompassing sweetness of Krishna. Devotees feel immense joy and bliss while singing this bhajan, as it brings them closer to the divine, experiencing his love and grace.

7. Govind Mero Hai

गोविंद मेरो है, गोपाल मेरो है।

सुन लो मेरे प्रभु, सारा भार तेरो है।

This bhajan means "Govind is mine, Gopal is mine" and is a declaration of the devotee's unwavering faith and devotion to Krishna. It expresses the belief that Krishna is the protector and caretaker of the devotee. By surrendering all burdens to Krishna, the devotee finds solace and comfort. Singing this bhajan fosters a sense of trust and security, as devotees feel Krishna's loving presence in their lives, guiding and supporting them through all challenges.

8. Nazar Mein Rahte Ho

नज़र में रहते हो तुम, दिल में बसते हो तुम।

ये तुमसे कह दूँ अभी, या ना कह दूँ कभी।

This bhajan means "You are in my sight, you dwell in my heart." It conveys the intimate and personal relationship between the devotee and Krishna. The lyrics reflect the devotee's deep longing and love for Krishna, acknowledging his omnipresence and the continuous impact he has on their life. Singing this bhajan evokes feelings of closeness and emotional connection with Krishna, reinforcing the belief that he is always watching over and caring for his devotees.

9. O Mere Banke Bihari Lal

ओ मेरे बाँके बिहारी लाल,

तेरे दरस बिना मोहे ना लगे मोहे कोई काम।

This bhajan means "O my charming Bihari Lal, without your sight, nothing feels worthwhile to me." It reflects the deep yearning and devotion of the devotee for Krishna's divine vision (darshan). The bhajan highlights the enchanting beauty and playful nature of Krishna, especially in his role as the beloved of the gopis. Singing this bhajan fills devotees with a sense of longing and love, as they seek the divine presence and grace of Krishna in their lives.

"O Mere Banke Bihari Lal Tum Itna Na Karo Shringar Nazar Lag Jayegi" is a popular bhajan that expresses the deep love and adoration devotees have for Lord Krishna, often visualized as Banke Bihari, the charming and playful form of Krishna in Vrundavan.

10. Mira Ke Prabhu Girdhar Nagar

मीरा के प्रभु गिरधर नागर,

राधा के मनमोहन।

These lines mean "Mira's Lord is Girdhar Nagar, is a name for Krishna, referring to his act of lifting the Govardhan Hill to protect the people of Vrundavan. Invoking this name in the bhajan reminds devotees of Krishna's omnipotence and his benevolent care for all who seek his refuge.

"Radha Ke Manmohan" means "the one who enchants Radha," emphasizing Krishna's deep and loving relationship with Radha. It encourages devotees to cultivate a similar love and devotion towards Krishna, aspiring for a deep and personal connection with him.

These bhajans, through their beautiful lyrics and soulful melodies, serve as powerful tools for devotees to express their love, faith, and longing for Krishna. Each bhajan encapsulates different aspects of Krishna's divine personality and the various ways devotees connect with him. Singing and listening to these bhajans not only enriches one's spiritual practice but also brings immense joy, peace, and a deeper connection to the divine presence of Lord Krishna.

Bhajans are a powerful medium to experience and express devotion to Krishna. They elevate the soul, purify the heart, and foster a deep, personal connection with the divine. By incorporating bhajans into daily practice, devotees can enhance their spiritual journey, cultivate inner peace, and unite with fellow devotees in shared love for Krishna.

Community and Satsang in Krishna Bhakti

Joining Krishna Bhakti Communities

Krishna Bhakti communities provide a supportive environment for devotees to deepen their spiritual practice. These communities offer a place to connect with like-minded individuals who share a love for Krishna. Being part of such a community can enhance one's spiritual journey through shared experiences, collective worship, and mutual encouragement. Many temples and spiritual organizations around the world, such as ISKCON (International Society for Krishna Consciousness), Bhakti Centers, and local Vaishnava groups, welcome new members and provide various resources for spiritual growth.

Participating in Satsangs

Satsang, a Sanskrit word meaning "association with truth." It is a fundamental practice in Krishna Bhakti. These gatherings typically involve chanting (kirtan), listening to spiritual discourses (pravachan), and engaging in discussions about Krishna's teachings and His devine pastimes (leelas).

- Kirtan: Participating in collective kirtan allows devotees to immerse themselves in the holy names of Krishna. This is considered one of the most potent forms of devotion. The collective energy and devotion in a kirtan can elevate the spirit. It brings joy and a deep sense of connection with Krishna.
- Listening to Discourses: Spiritual discourses offer insights into the teachings of Krishna. These are found in sacred texts like the Bhagavad Gita and Srimad Bhagavatam. These talks are often given by experienced teachers or advanced practitioners. They help in deepening the understanding by providing practical guidance for living a Krishna-centered life.
- Engaging in Discussions: Satsangs provide an opportunity to clarify doubts by open discussions and

question-and-answer sessions. It also provides a platform to share personal experiences, and gain new perspectives on Krishna's pastimes and teachings. This interactive learning helps in developing a sense of belongingness and collective wisdom.

- Spiritual Support: Being part of a community offers emotional and spiritual support, helping individuals stay committed to their practice.
- Shared Learning: Learning from others' experiences and insights can deepen one's own understanding and appreciation of Krishna's teachings.
- Enhanced Devotion: Regular participation in satsangs and community activities can strengthen one's devotion and keep the mind focused on spiritual goals.

Overall, joining Krishna Bhakti communities and participating in satsangs enriches the spiritual journey. This journey offers a path of love, learning, and shared devotion towards Krishna.

Chapter 6: Ending it up

Krishna, known by various names reflecting his divine qualities and attributes, inspires devotion and reverence among His devotees through His myriad leelas. Each name carries profound meanings and symbolizes different aspects of Krishna's personality and role in the universe. Through His leelas, Krishna reveals His divine nature, teaches eternal truths, and demonstrates His boundless love and compassion for all beings.

From childhood to adulthood, from Vrundavan to Kurukshetra, Krishna's leelas are timeless stories that continue to captivate hearts and minds. Whether as a mischievous child stealing butter, a fearless warrior guiding Arjuna on the battlefield, or the supreme teacher expounding spiritual wisdom in the Bhagavad Gita, Krishna's leelas illustrate the multifaceted nature of the divine and its relevance to human life.

Devotees invoke Krishna's names in prayer, meditation, and contemplation to deepen their spiritual connection and seek his blessings. Each leela provides profound insights into the nature of divinity, the principles of righteousness and devotion, and the eternal bond between the Supreme and his devotees.

Krishna's leelas continue to inspire people across generations and cultures, serving as a guiding light on the path of righteousness, love, and spiritual enlightenment. Through these divine stories, devotees aspire to emulate Krishna's virtues, deepen their devotion, and ultimately, attain union with the divine.

Thus, the leelas of Krishna are not mere stories but profound teachings that illuminate the path of bhakti (devotion) and spiritual realization, offering solace, inspiration, and divine guidance to all who seek the eternal truth.

The various leelas associated with Krishna's names—Madan, Madhusudan, Manmohan, Manohar, Mayura, Murlidhar, and Muralimanohar—each highlight different aspects of his divine nature and the profound spiritual teachings they convey. From the enchanting beauty that captivates the hearts of devotees to the heroic acts of vanquishing evil, Krishna's leelas offer a rich tapestry of stories that inspire love, devotion, and a deeper understanding of the divine.

These leelas serve as a reminder that the divine can manifest in various forms and actions, each carrying its own unique significance and lessons. By meditating on these stories and invoking Krishna by his different names, devotees can connect with the different facets of his divinity, experiencing the joy, protection, and spiritual growth that comes from a deep and personal relationship with the divine.

In each leela, Krishna's interactions with his devotees underscore the importance of love, surrender, and devotion as the foundation of spiritual practice. Whether through his playful antics, his enchanting music, or his heroic deeds, Krishna continues to captivate the hearts and minds of his devotees, leading them on a path of spiritual awakening and fulfillment.

These leelas of Krishna not only illustrate the significance of his various names but also convey profound spiritual teachings. Each leela exemplifies different aspects of Krishna's divine nature, from his wondrous and unconquerable qualities to his infinite bliss, playful nature, compassionate leadership, and boundless mercy. Through these stories, devotees can deepen their understanding and connection with Krishna, experiencing the divine love and protection that he embodies.

These leelas of Krishna not only highlight the significance of his various names but also convey profound spiritual teachings. Each leela exemplifies different aspects of Krishna's divine nature, from his roles as protector and guide to his playful and enchanting qualities. Through these stories, devotees can deepen their understanding and connection with Krishna, experiencing the divine love, protection, and wisdom that he embodies.

Verses Kindler Publication

Verses Kindler Publication

Reach us through our website -
https://www.verseskindlerpublication.com/
For more information visit our Instagram or Facebook page.